Edward Fletcher's

Non-Dating Price Guide to Bottles, Pipes and Dolls' Heads

Edward Fletcher's
Non-Dating Price Guide to Bottles, Pipes and Dolls' Heads

BLANDFORD PRESS

POOLE   DORSET

First published 1976
by Blandford Press Ltd,
Link House, West Street, Poole, Dorset BH15 1LL

Copyright © Edward Fletcher 1976

ISBN 0 7137 0781 X

Printed in Great Britain by Staples Printers
and bound by Robert Hartnoll Ltd

CONTENTS

Introduction   7
1. Internally-stoppered Bottles   11
2. Ginger Beers   90
3. Inks   92
4. Bitters   94
5. Sealed Bottles   96
6. Case Gins and Schnapps   102
7. Black Whiskies, Seltzers and Ginger Beers   104
8. Fire Grenades   106
9. Patent Medicines   108
10. Poisons   112
11. Glass Figurals   114
12. Fairy Lights   116
13. Baby Feeders   118
14. Ointment Pots   121
15. Cream Jugs   122
16. Hot Water Bottles   123
17. Historical Stoneware Flasks and Jugs   124
18. Transfer-printed Stoneware Whiskies   127
19. Clay Tobacco Pipes   128
20. Dolls' Heads and Limbs   129
21. Pot Lids   130
Bibliography: Books and Magazines   132
Bottle Shops and Dealers   133

Author's Note

As the specification drawings taken from the Patent Office Records have been reproduced facsimile in their original sizes, completely accurate line definition has not always been possible. The number shown in bold type before the name of each inventor is the original patent application number. Readers who wish to consult the complete specification and the inventor's original drawings should quote that number and the year in which it was issued when visiting or writing to the Patent Office, Chancery Lane, London.

INTRODUCTION

In my previous book, *International Bottle Collecters' Guide* I offered advice on buying and selling bottles in Britain, North America, and Australia and I used a numerical scale to compare the rarity, value and collectability of bottles found in different countries. It was necessary to use such a scale because in these present inflationary times any comparisons between the bottles of one country and another expressed in currencies would have been out of date before the book went to press. The advantage of my numerical scale is that no matter what effects the ups and downs of dollars and pounds have on bottle prices the relative values of the numbers on the scale remain constant.

This present book is an attempt to compile a guide to the rarity, value and collectability of the best of Britain's Victorian dump finds using the same numerical scale. It is *not* a *price list* covering every bottle, clay tobacco pipe, pot lid and doll's head found by British diggers. Such a list would be wastefully repetitious and out of date in a very short time because dump finds which differ only slightly in embossing, shape, size or colour *usually* have the same value and because new discoveries are being made every day. Finds which can be made by the most inexperienced newcomer to dump digging have been omitted because they are objects which ought to be dug up rather than bought. (My earlier books, *Bottle Collecting* and *A Treasure Hunter's Guide* gave full details on how and where to find them.) Once these common finds have been made by digging you can turn with a greater appreciation of rarity and collectability to buying more valuable bottles.

You will not have to pay high prices for all of them. This guide includes many bottles and other objects which can at present be bought quite cheaply. They merit inclusion here

7

because their rarity is not yet widely appreciated or because their values will greatly increase when they become part of a specialised collection. The hobby is still in its infancy in Britain and there are numerous bargains to be found on dealers' shelves and at bottle auctions by those armed with a little knowledge of the subject. I wholeheartedly recommend specialisation in those bottles included in this book which have been given a low price guide number to any reader who finds the cost of bottles at the upper end of the scale beyond his budget.

A writer who attempts a price guide to a hobby largely concerned with digging up objects buried for a hundred years and more faces a task similar to that of someone putting together a jigsaw puzzle from which a substantial number of pieces are missing. Less than one quarter of all accessible nineteenth century refuse dumps in Britain have been excavated and there is no doubt the undug sites contain examples of bottles, pipes, pot lids and dolls' heads which have not seen light of day since many a great-grandparent was born. For this reason a totally comprehensive guide to the contents of Britain's nineteenth century refuse dumps is an impossible scheme at the present time and even a selective guide such as this must be accepted by writer and readers as the best that can be achieved on the evidence brought to light up to the time of writing. The finds already made by dump diggers provide enough pieces of the bottle collecting jigsaw to let us see the general appearance of the picture which will emerge when all the pieces are found. Above ground evidence gleaned from nineteenth century newspaper advertisements and other sources helps shade in the blank areas and enables us to make informed guesses about finds yet to come.

Regular readers of the magazine, *Bottles and Relics News* and the newsletters issued by the British Bottle Collectors Club will recognise in the following pages extracts from many of my previously published articles, pamphlets and booklets. Their republication in this book has enabled me to update the information they contained, to convert prices originally quoted in pounds and pence—and now out of date—to my non-dating numerical scale, and to bring together in a single volume all earlier attempts at assessing the rarity, value and collectability of finds made by members of the British Bottle

8

Collectors Club. Many new facts and finds have been brought to light by the research and digging efforts of club members during the past year and they are published here for the first time. Together with numerous drawings and photographs the whole forms a book which all bottle collectors—tiros and old hands at the game—will find invaluable when buying or selling.

Overseas readers who have not yet read *International Bottle Collecters' Guide* should experience little difficulty in translating the numerical price guide in this book to the currency of their own country. A number of bottles dealt with here are found wherever dump digging has become a popular hobby. Ascertain the present selling price of one of these bottles in your country and you will then be able to gauge the selling price of any other British bottle mentioned in the book by dividing one price guide number by another. All readers, British and foreign, should note that I refer throughout this book to bottles in mint dug condition. To qualify for that category a bottle excavated from a dump must have no cracks, no chips or flakes of glass missing from lip, neck, body or base, and its surfaces must retain ninety per cent of their original shine. The overwhelming majority of bottle collectors regard mint dug bottles as the only specimens worthy of a price tag. I am on the side of the majority.

Edward Fletcher,
Redcar, Cleveland, 1976

1. INTERNALLY-STOPPERED BOTTLES

Thanks to searches made by British Bottle Collectors Club members at the Patent Office in London we now have a complete record of all internally-stoppered mineral water bottles patented in Britain between 1868 and 1907. Although these records include details of many ideas for bottles which developed no further than the inventors' drawing boards they do provide evidence about the basic workings of all those which reached production stage. This is the *only* group of British bottles for which we have a complete record and for that reason alone all collectors ought to be grateful to those who spent their time tracking down the patent specifications. However, even these valuable records have their short-comings. They do not tell us which manufacturers used dark green, brown, amber and blue glass to make the bottles; nor do they tell us conclusively which bottles progressed from drawing board to production stage. We must rely almost entirely on digging evidence to provide that information and in the case of internally-stoppered bottles this evidence lags considerably behind research evidence. Before discussing the various internally-stoppered bottles which have been found let me provide readers with the complete record of patented closures.

Although it is generally accepted in bottle collecting circles that the era of the internal stopper began on 3 September 1872 when Hiram Codd perfected the globe-stoppered and crimp-necked bottle for which he will always be remembered, other inventors were at work on improved closures for mineral water bottles several years earlier. The majority attempted to introduce an elastic ball into the neck of a Hamilton bottle and to devise a method of moving the ball to pour the contents. The first important breakaway from this approach came in 1868 with the Adams and Barrett wooden plug. This was followed in 1870 by L. Rose and his piston stopper which carried an india-rubber washer that fitted tightly into the neck of the bottle. In the following year the Kilner Brothers suggested a glass ball stopper for use in a bottle with a conical rubber ring in its neck which was held in place by a metal cap and secured by wire.

Henry Barrett, now in partnership with Charles Elers, developed his plug stopper a stage further in 1871 by fitting a valve. A similar idea was put forward by H. Aylesbury in January 1872, and by Trotman and Price, who also added a ring-pull, in September of the same year. By a remarkable coincidence their patent application is dated 3 September—the very day on which Hiram Codd perfected the Codd bottle. On the following day C. Tapp applied for a patent on his conical plug stopper—an indication of the fierce competition for mineral water bottle sales which was about to commence! Leon Vallet is also mentioned in the records for that year; he sought provisional protection on 17 December for his first internal stopper invention. Full details of all the above inventions together with the various patents sought by Hiram Codd during development of his bottle are now given.

1868

2708. Adams, J., and **Barrett, H.** Sept. 2. *Disclaimer.*

FIG. 5.

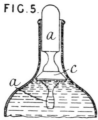

Stoppers, internal, for bottles containing aërated or other gaseous liquids. A plug *a*, of wood having a greater specific gravity than water, is formed near its lower end with an inclined groove for receiving an india-rubber washer *c*. The stopper having been passed into the neck, the bottle is filled in an inverted position, and the stopper sinks through the liquid into the neck. The internal pressure then forces the washer firmly against the surface of the neck.

Bottling.—For filling the bottle with aerated liquid, the bottle is inverted and held in a rest; an air tube, actuated by a treadle, is then passed up into the bottle, and the liquid is pumped in through another pipe. The air escapes through the air tube, the pressure being determined by a weighted valve in the tube. The stopper sinks through the liquid as described above, and closes the bottle as it is removed from the bottling-machine.

1870

1639. Rose, L. June 7.
[*Provisional protection only.*]

Stoppers, internal. A stopper for bottles containing aërated liquids &c. consists of a piston or rod carrying at its lower end a disc or washer of india-rubber or other suitable substance. The diameter of the piston is nearly equal to the opening in the neck, "space being allowed for the "passage of the gas and water or other liquid used "in the manufacture." The piston is suspended in the neck and held in its position by a ring, disc, or cross-bar. The washer is of such diameter as to fit tightly the upper part of the neck when the piston is forced up by the internal pressure. The stopper is extracted by the aid of the ring attached to its upper end.

3070. Codd, H. Nov. 24.
Amended.

Stoppers.—The first part of the invention relates to the construction of bottle necks with transverse passages for stoppering them. At the top of the bottle is a head piece having a transverse hole through it at right-angles to, but communicating with, the hole in the neck. The cork or stopper fits in the transverse hole. The second part consists in stoppering bottles which contain aërated liquids, by means of either ground glass stoppers, or balls of glass, wood, cork, india-rubber, or gutta-percha. When ground glass stoppers are employed, a long tapering glass stopper, carefully ground, is placed within the body of the bottle in the process of manufacture, the smaller end towards the neck, and the passage in

the neck is suitably ground to receive the stopper. When loose balls are employed, the bottle is made with an annular groove in the inside of the upper end of the neck, and closely fitting therein is placed a ring of cork, india-rubber, or gutta-percha, of such thickness that about half the ring will project beyond the mouth of the groove and prevent the ball within the bottle from passing it. To empty the bottle, the stem of the stopper or the ball is pressed down by a lever or other mechanical means.

1871

2212. Codd, H. Aug. 22.

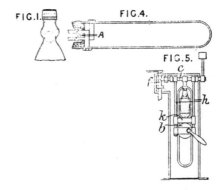

Bottle necks.—In bottles fitted with internal ball stoppers such as are described in Specification No. 3070, A.D. 1870, a recess is made in the neck to retain the stopper while the contents are being poured out. Fig. 1 shows one form of the neck. The contraction is formed by pressing in the sides so that the neck at that part assumes an oval form. Above the contraction the neck is widened to form a recess, into which the stopper rolls when the liquid is being poured out.

13

Bottle necks, making.—The tongs employed for shaping the outsides of the necks of bottles are fitted with arms having projections A, Fig. 4, for making the internal groove in which the washer of cork or india-rubber is placed to form the seating for the internal ball stopper. The arms beccme closed together when the limbs of the tongs are separated, and *vice versa.*

Bottling.—For filling internally-stoppered bottles with aërated liquids, the apparatus shown in Fig. 5 is employed. The bottle rests on a piece *k*, which can slide on arms *h* swinging from a hollow shaft *c*, and is pressed up to the filling-nozzle on the same shaft by an eccentric *b* rotated by a handle. The liquid is supplied through the hollow shaft *c* from the pipe *f*. When the bottle is filled, it is inverted by turning the shaft *c* in its bearings, so that the stopper will fall on to its seat before the bottle is removed from the nozzle.

2882. Kilner, C., and Kilner, T. Oct. 27. [*Provisional protection only.*]

Stoppers.—For stoppering ginger beer and other aërated water bottles, a ball of glass or other suitable material is put into the bottle, and a ring or washer is fitted into the neck. The inner circumference of the washer is of a conical form, the larger opening being towards ·the interior of the bottle. The washer is held in its place by a metallic cap, placed on the ring or neck of the bottle and secured by wire. The bottle, after being filled, is inverted so that the ball falls towards the neck; the gas within the bottle then keeps the ball pressed up against the conical surface of the washer.

3484. Barrett, H. and Elers, C. G. Dec. 23.

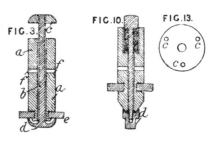

Stoppers for bottles containing gaseous or aërated liquids are made of material sufficiently heavy to sink in the liquid in the bottle. In the form shown in Fig. 3, the stopper consists of a cylinder *a* fitted at its lower end with an elastic washer *e*, which, when the bottle is inverted after being filled, seats itself against the lower part of the bottle neck. A valve *d* is forced by the internal pressure against the washer and prevents escape of the contents. When the bottle is to be opened, the valve *d* is moved from its seat by depressing the valve stem *b* by means of a knob *c*, which projects from the mouth of the bottle. The compressed gas in the bottle then escapes through the central hole in the stopper and through side holes *f*. The stopper, being thus relieved of pressure, will fall into the bottle. Fig. 10 shows another form, in which the valve *d*, instead of being seated on the washer, fits against the lower end of the stopper; the knob at the upper end of the valve stem may rest on a rubber or other spring. The invention also comprises a washer, shown in Fig. 13, having three or more holes *c* formed in it. When the stopper to which this washer is attached is pressed down, the central part of the washer is moved

14

away from its seat at the base of the bottle neck, and the holes c, being thus uncovered, allow the escape of gas.

1872

248. Aylesbury, H. Jan. 25.

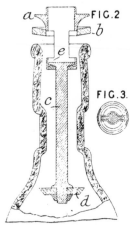

Stoppers.—Relates to plug stoppers particularly adapted for bottles containing aërated liquids. The plug is hollow and lantern-shaped or open sided for part of its length; near the top is a flange a, Fig. 2, the under side of which is made the same shape as the neck of the bottle. An india-rubber washer b forms an airtight joint. A sliding rod c, passing through the bottom of the plug, carries at its lower end an india-rubber washer d; for part of its upper length the rod is formed with one or two feathers. Fig. 3, terminates in a disc e, which slides in the hole in the plug. To fill the bottle, the washer d is pushed below the root of the neck; the liquid is then admitted, and the pressure forces the washer d against the neck, forming a tight joint. At the same time, the disc e rises to the top of the plug, disengaging the feathers from the hole at the bottom of the plug. On turning the plug by the flange a, the lower ends of the feathers abut against the bottom of the plug, thus locking the stopper. In a modification, the sliding rod is replaced by a rod screwed through the hole in the plug, the raising and lowering being effected by turning the plug.

2611. Trotman, F., and Price, G. B. Sept. 3.

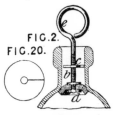

Stoppers.—A rod b carries at its lower end a vulcanized india-rubber washer d between two metal plates, the upper plate being smaller than the lower one. The rod carries one or more guides c, and its upper end terminates in a ring or knob e, which will not pass through the neck of the bottle. The rod may be bent so that its middle portion forms a guide, or so that both ends are fixed into the metal plates, or so that a wedge may be thrust in between the ring and the mouth of the bottle. The rod, with its ring handle and a hole for a locking pin or wedge, may be stamped out of sheet metal. A printed or stamped, or ornamented disc of cardboard or metal, Fig. 20, may be used as a label.

2621. Codd, H. Sept. 3.

Bottle necks; bottle necks, making.—In the neck of a bottle for aërated liquids are formed inclined

15

projecting ridges *d, d*, Fig. 1, one on each side, and the lower part of the neck *c* is contracted. When the ball stopper *a* is pushed in to open the bottle, it rolls down the projecting ridges till it is stopped by the

FIG I.

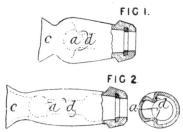

FIG 2

contraction. It is then allowed to roll to the opposite side of the ridges *d*, which prevent it from returning when the bottle is inclined for pouring the liquid. The moulds, in which the bottles are blown, are formed with projections to produce the ridges *d* in the neck when the bottle is blown. In a modification, Fig. 2, the lower part of the internal projecting ridges *d* is curved. The stopper *a*, when the bottle is inclined, is prevented from returning to the mouth by the curved portions of the projecting ridges *d*. If the stopper is made with a stem, the stem may be made much shorter when using the inclined ridges.

2634. Tapp, C. Sept. 4.

Stoppers.—A conical plug *a* of glass, earthenware, &c. is just large enough at its base to pass through the neck of the bottle, and carries an india-rubber ring *b*. The plug may have a head *c* at its smaller end, or it may be attached to a cord or wire *d* connected to the mouth of the bottle. An ellipsoidal plug, and a flat disc of india-rubber sprung over the head and fitting close around the neck of the plug, may be used or the ring may fit in a circular groove in the neck of the bottle. The stopper *a* is

FIG.4.

passed into the bottle with the ring *b* at the smallest part, and is held suspended in the bottle by the cord *d*, whilst the ring *b* is pushed along the plug by a pair of tongs, or by a rod, or tube, until it is at the middle of the plug. When the stopper is pulled up into the neck of the bottle, it is retained by the pressure of the gas.

3828. Vallet, L. Dec. 17. [*Provisional protection only.*]

Stoppers; opening internally-stoppered bottles.—Relates to bottles for holding soda water, ginger beer, lemonade, and other similar liquids. The neck is formed with an annular recess at about the middle of its length, in order to receive a coiled spring which is wound around a hollow piston. The piston has side projections which fit into guide grooves in the neck.

The inventions patented during the years 1873-1876 fall roughly into three categories:

1. Improvements to original ideas by the important names

in the field. (Especially Codd and Vallet.)

2. The products of a number of imitators who made minor (yet sometimes important) changes to the basic designs invented by Codd and by Barrett and Elers.

3. The emergence of several new names in closure invention—notably John Lamont, Leon Vallet, Sutcliffe & Fewings, Breffit & Edwards, and Hunt & Gledhill. All in this group developed workable closures which were widely used by the mineral water trade, though the Hunt & Gledhill idea was only popular in Australia where, for many years, it outsold bottles using Codd, Barrett & Elers, and other closures.

Details of all developments during this period are given below:

1873

97. Thwaites, R., and Stephens, L. A. Jan.9.

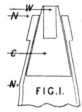

FIG.1.

Corks, retaining; stoppers.—A bottle for enclosing aërated liquids and beverages has the inside upper part of the neck N made to taper upwards, as in Fig. 1. The cork C, made by preference from cork wood, is also made conical, the vertical angle being slightly greater than that of the bottle neck, so that the larger end of the cork may grip first in the neck. The smaller end of the cork is weighted, either by inserting a piece of lead W, or by fixing it to a cap, tip, or knob, or a ring or hook, so that the smaller end is the heavier, and the whole cork will sink in the liquid. The cork is forced into the bottle by means of an inverted cone or funnel made to fit over the mouth;

the bottle is filled usually in an inverted position, and the cork is then drawn into the neck by means of the ring or knob. To prevent the cork from falling back into the bottle, a wire or pin is passed through the cork over the mouth of the bottle; or, a catch may be fixed to the cork, and form part of the weight.

1939. Risque, E. D. May 29.

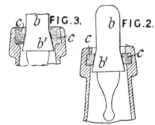

Stoppers.—Relates to the construction of bottle necks and stoppers. The neck of the bottle is made with an annular recess, which is fitted with a ring c, Fig. 2, of cork, after the stopper has been inserted. The ring c, Fig. 3, is fixed by means of cement. The stopper is made of lignum vitae or other heavy wood, the upper part *b* being made cylindrical and the lower part b^1 conical. The stopper is long enough to prevent it from turning over inside the bottle. The conical part b^1 fits up to the bevelled washer *c*, and is kept there by the pressure of gas in the bottle.

4252. Horner, F., Horner, W. W., and Sibley, J. Dec. 27.

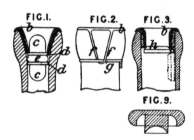

FIG.1.   FIG.2.   FIG.3.

FIG.9.

Stoppers for bottles containing aërated liquids &c. are formed of a plug *c*, Fig. 1, having an enlarged part *e* in the middle, and a groove at each side of this part to receive a washer *d*. Either washer bears against a ring *b*, which may be secured in the neck by cement, or by loops *f* and a wire *g*, Fig. 2, cork or other yielding material being in this case placed between the ring and the neck. In another form, a disc *h*, Fig. 3, is hinged to the ring.

Opening internally-stoppered bottles.—Fig. 9 shows an instrument for pressing in the stopper.

4268. Codd, H., and Foster, F. Dec. 29.

Stoppers.—The neck is made with V-shaped ring grooves, Figs. 5 and 9, into which is pressed a strip or ring of cork or the like, to form a washer for the stopper to bear against. If the bottle is to contain aërated or non-aërated liquids, the stopper is form-

ed as shown in Fig. 5, but, if it is to contain aërated liquids only, the stopper may have either of the forms shown in Figs. 9, 10, 11, 12, 13, and 14.

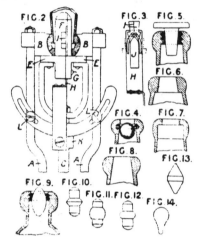

FIG.2.   FIG.3.   FIG.5.
FIG.6.
FIG.4.   FIG.7.
FIG.8.
FIG.9.   FIG.10.
FIG.11. FIG.12   FIG.13.
FIG.14.

1874

108. Vernon, W. J. Jan. 8.

FIG.1.

Stoppering; stoppers.—In filling aërated-liquid bottles having light internal stoppers, means are provided for causing the stoppers to sink on to their seatings while the bottle is held in the inverted position as usual. For this purpose, the stoppers *c* are loaded by weights *b* attached by clips *a*.

406. Read, G. Feb. 2.

Stoppers.—A stopper for a bottle containing aërated liquids consists

18

of a plug of metal, wood, cork, glass, porcelain, &c., covered at one end with a taper tube of india-rubber or other material, as shown in Fig. 5.

FIG. 5.

The plug and the tube are inserted into the bottle, and the tube is drawn over the plug by means of two wires, one having a loop at one end and a handle at the other. The loop passes under the thin end of the tube, which, by means of the other wire, is pulled over the end of the plug. The wires are then withdrawn, leaving in the bottle the covered plug of greater diameter than the orifice of the neck of the bottle.

700. Hunt, E., [*Gledhill, G.*]. Feb. 24.

FIG. 1. FIG. 2.

Stoppers; bottle necks, making.— The stopper A, Fig. 1, of an aërated water bottle is a ball of india-rubber of such density that it will sink in the liquid when free to do so. The outlet of the bottle is a short thickened nozzle, with a spherical seating for the stopper, and a concave shoulder to receive the stopper while the contents of the bottle are being poured out. The stopper may be forced in through the outlet of the bottle through a taper tube with a mandrel, or by water pressure. Fig. 2 shows the nozzle of the glass bottle as first formed in the mould. To finish the bottle, it is held in a cup-shaped ponty, and the nozzle is heated and brought to the shape shown in Fig. 1, by a hand-tool, a ring of metal being added if necessary.

1923. Lamont, J. June 2.

Bottle necks, making; stoppers.— Relates to the construction of necks and stoppers for glass and earthenware bottles to contain aërated liquids. The bottle is made with a flange or rim inside the mouth, by means of an expanding mandrel shown in Fig. 3, consisting of two shaped pieces a formed on the end of two springs a^1 attached at a^{11} to the central spindle h of the hand tool, to which is also attached an end disc b^1 to form the end of the bottle neck. The two blocks c^1 for shaping the outside of the neck are fixed on a double spring c, c^x, which is attached to the spindle b by screw nuts. When the spring sides c^x are pressed inwards, the parts a of the mandrel are forced out by the pins a^{111}.

*Stoppers.—*The stopper consists of a glass, porcelain, or heavy hard-wood plug C, Fig. 5, fitted with an india-rubber ring or washer B. The plug is first dropped into the bottle, and the washer is then forced down into the groove by a split tube, which takes over one end of the plug. To lighten the stopper, the plug may be grooved; the ends of the plug may be fitted with india-rubber caps, to prevent the stopper from breaking the bottle. The plug may also be made of an elliptical or spherical shape, the washer being sprung on before inserting the stopper. The washer may be made thin enough to bend to the shape of the neck. The stopper may consist of a ball of india-rubber made with a central core of heavy material. In a different construction of stopper, for a bottle

19

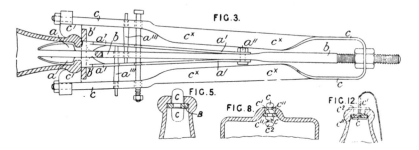

FIG. 3.

FIG. 5.

FIG. 8.

FIG. 12.

having a flat square rim inside, an oval metal disc c, Fig. 12, is provided with a screw stem c^1, to the top of which a chain or wire is attached. An india-rubber washer is screwed down close to the disc by a thin metallic nut c^{11}. When this stopper is inserted and the bottle is filled the stopper is drawn up by the wire until the washer bears against the rim, a large nut c^2 being screwed on to the stem until it draws the washer tight against the rim. By these means of stoppering, bottles with short necks may be used; or, the stoppers may be applied to bottles without necks, as shown in Fig. 8.

3448. Codd, H. Oct. 8.

Bottles; stoppers.—In making earthenware bottles for containing aërated or effervescing liquids, the bottle is moulded from clay in the ordinary manner, and is allowed to dry for a few days; it is then placed in a lathe, and a groove, to receive an elastic washer, is cut round the inside of the neck. A ball of clay, in a drier state than the clay forming the bottle, is dropped in, and the bottle and stopper are further dried until they are ready for making or burning. The shoulder of the bottle is made at right-angles to the body to prevent the ball from rolling back

when the bottle is being emptied; or the neck may be shaped as described in the Specifications of the inventor's former patents.

3546. Fox, H. B. Oct. 15.

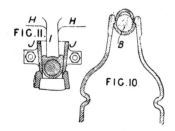

FIG. 11.

FIG. 10.

Stoppers; bottles.—A stopper for a bottle containing aërated liquid consists of a ball B, Fig. 10, of metal, stone, or heavy hard substance, loosely encased in india-rubber, cork, or other elastic material. The bottle is formed with a tapered neck, and with a ridge to form a seat for the stopper. A V-shaped, zig-zag, or corrugated ridge is also formed inside the bottle, to prevent the stopper from running into the neck while the contents are being poured out. An instrument for placing the stopper in the bottle consists of a fixed taper tube J, Fig. 11, through which the ball is forced by a plunger 1.

20

3815. Edwards, J. Nov. 5.

Bottles.—In order to retain an internal stopper while pouring, an aërated water bottle is formed with a chamber A, Figs. 1 and 2, into which the stopper falls. Fig. 1 shows the form of chamber for an ordinary soda-water bottle. A globular bottle is provided with a chamber A similar to that shown in Fig. 2.

3855. Froggatt, W., and **Ballard, J.** Nov. 9.

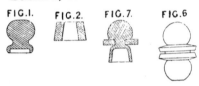

Stoppers.—An internal stopper for an aërated water bottle consists of a block tin, glass, porcelain, chinaware, mineral ivory, or mineral spar stud provided with one or two india-rubber washers. Fig. 1 shows one form of stud, the washer for which is shown in Fig. 2. A double stopper, with a middle neck on each side of which there is a flat washer, is shown in Fig. 6. Fig. 7 shows a third form of stud provided with a flat washer. The stud may be square in section. The stud is first passed into the bottle and the washer is then placed on it by means of a pair of tongs.

4333. King, A. Dec. 16.

Stoppers.—Internal stoppers for bottles containing aërated liquids are made of light material, so that they will float in the liquid. In the form shown in Fig. 2, the stopper consists of a wooden top *c*, Fig. 2,

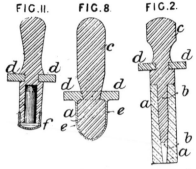

fitted into a lower cork portion *a*. An india-rubber washer *d* is fitted in a groove in the top portion. An india-rubber capsule *e*, Fig. 8, formed with the washer *d*, may be used to protect the wood from the action of the liquid or gas. The stopper may be made hollow from metal or other material; or, it may be made entirely of wood, the lower part being made hollow and covered by a screwed metal cap *f*, as shown in Fig. 11. The bottle is filled in the upright position, the stopper rising on the liquid into the neck of the bottle.

1875

53. Bowman, J. Jan. 6.

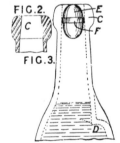

Stoppers; bottles.—The neck of a bottle for containing aërated liquids is made conical, as shown at C, Fig. 2, to receive the internal stopper E, Fig. 3. The stopper is made egg-shaped or otherwise, and is grooved to receive an india-rubber or other washer F, which is fixed in place after the stopper has been placed in the bottle. The bottle is formed with a shoulder D, to retain the stopper while the contents are being poured out.

262. Aylesbury, H. Jan. 23.

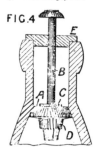
FIG.4
E
B
A C
D

Stoppers.—A stopper for a bottle containing aërated liquids consists of two india-rubber discs A, E, placed on a spindle B. The lower disc A is fixed to the rod by means of nuts C, D, while the upper disc or cap E is free to slide on the rod. The stopper is shown in position in Fig. 4. To pour out the contents of the bottle, the rod is depressed, so that the gas in escaping blows out the upper disc or cap E.

418. Wadsworth, J. Feb. 4.

Stoppers.—An internal stopper for a bottle containing aërated liquids consists of a plug A, Fig. 1, of pipe-clay, provided with an india-rubber washer B. In a modification, shown in Fig. 3, to facilitate the opening of the bottle, the plug is reduced in diameter between the two ends A, B, the reduced part *x* having

longitudinal grooves C for the immediate escape of gas when the stopper is depressed.

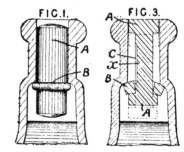
FIG.1.   FIG.3.
A
A   C
B   x
B
A

490. Vallet, L. Feb. 10.

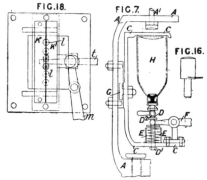
FIG.18.   FIG.7.
A'   A
C   C
H   FIG.16.
G
D
D'   F
E   E
C   D'   c
A

FIG.3.
b
b'   b'
d   d
e
c

Stoppers; opening internally-stoppered bottles.—An internal stopper for a bottle containing an aërated or gaseous liquid is made of heavy material such as tinned metal or Britannia metal, or of glass, china, or wood, &c., and consists of a short stem terminating at one end in a head *b*, Fig. 3, and at the other in a cone *c*. An india-rubber or other washer *e* is kept in place by a ridge *d*. Sometimes, the mouth of the bottle is closed by a small cork in addition to the stopper, in order to exclude dirt. The head *b* of the stopper may have a groove b^1 for a washer, which is put in position, after the stopper has been inserted in the bottle by means of the instrument shown in Fig. 14, or the modification shown in Fig. 15. In some cases, the stopper is enclosed in an india-rubber cap. In a modified stopper, the head *b* is dispensed with. Figs. 5 and 12 show

FIG.15.

FIG.14.

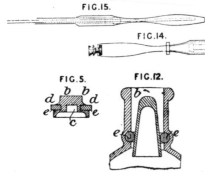

FIG.5.　　FIG.12.

other modifications, in the latter of which the washer *e* is placed in a groove in the bottle neck. An instrument for opening bottles provided with these stoppers is shown in Fig. 16. In a mould for casting metal stoppers, Fig. 18, cavities for a series of stoppers are formed between two blocks K, K¹, the metal being poured in through holes *l*. The cores are carried by a block which can be removed by a lever *t*, and the mould is opened by a lever *m*.

Bottling; stoppering.—The bottle H, Fig. 7, which is to be filled is carried by a frame *c*, which is pivoted to the main frame A by an adjustable bolt G. A tube D has a nozzle at each end, and can be pressed into the mouth of the bottle by a spring E acting on a collar. When the frame *c* is in the upright position, it can be raised by a

treadle-operated disc, so that the nozzle D at the end of the tube D enters the mouth of the supply pipe A¹. When the frame *c* is inverted, the stopper falls into the mouth of the bottle. The pipe D has an automatic valve D², and can be removed from the mouth of the bottle by a lever F. In a modified apparatus, the frame *c* has a bracket which projects over the mouth of the bottle, and the tube D slides in sockets in this bracket and in the head of the frame *c*, being moved by a lever as before.

2547. Catlow, U., and Hoyle, R. July 15.

FIG.I.　　FIG.2.

Stoppers; capsules, bottle.—The shank or core of a stopper for a bottle for effervescent liquids, beer, porter, or mineral waters, &c., is made of glass or earthenware &c., and is indented to enable it to hold a covering of india-rubber which is moulded on to it. The stopper may be double-ended, as shown in Fig. 1, or have an enlarged end covered with india-rubber, the other end having a hole to receive a string of porpoise hide &c., which is tied round the bottle neck or may be attached to a ring, or to a cork for excluding dirt from the bottle mouth. The india-rubber employed for covering the stopper is deodorized by washing in boiling caustic alkali. It is preferably first boiled in a solution of Canadian black ash, and then in a washing soda solution. The Provisional Specification states that dirt may be excluded from the bottle mouth by a paper capsule, which is pasted or tied in place.

3734. Vallet, L. Oct. 27.

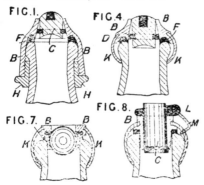

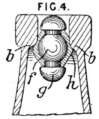

Stoppers.—To form a seating for an internal stopper C, Fig. 1, preferably that described in Specification No. 490, A.D. 1875, a dome-shaped, convex, or conical cap or cover B of Britannia metal, tinned metal, or of other metal, glass, earthenware, &c., is fitted on the neck of the bottle, and the joint between the cap and neck is formed of india-rubber, cork, leather, or other packing F. The cap may be screwed on an external thread on the neck, or on a split ring H surrounding the neck. The cap is preferably secured by wire K, Fig. 4, passing through holes in lugs on the cap B and fastened round the bottle neck. The elastic washer D on the stopper may be dispensed with, and the stopper then presses against the washer F. A cork piece may be inserted in the opening in the cap B, to keep dirt out of the bottle. In a modification, the cap B, Fig. 7, is formed in two pieces, and is secured by a wire K. When the bottle does not

contain aërated liquids, a wedge or tapered pin L, Fig. 8, is inserted in a hole in the stopper C, to jam it against the inner surface of the cap B. The pin may be secured to the stopper by a cord or chain M.

3751. Sutcliffe, T., and **Fewings, J.** Oct. 28.

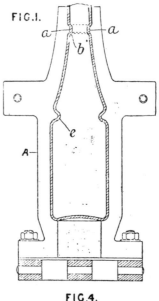

Stoppers; bottles; bottling.—A bottle for containing aërated liquids is blown in a mould A, Fig. 1, formed with a projection *a* for producing a corresponding internal projection or seat *b* in the neck for retaining an internal stopper, instead of forming the internal seat *b* simultaneously

24

with the mouth by special tools after the bottle is blown. After the part above the projection *b* is broken off, a ring is cast around the part *b* of the neck, and the mouth is worked into the form shown in Fig. 4. The bottle is also formed with an internal annular projection *e*, Fig. 1, for retaining the stopper while pouring out the contents, and for preventing the violent descent of the stopper. The stopper *f*, Fig. 4, is preferably shaped as shown. According to the Provisional Specification, an internal annular recess may be used instead of the projection *e*; or the projection or the recess may be duplicated. In some cases, a shoulder is formed between the conical part of the bottle and the top of the cylindrical part. In order that either end of the stopper may fit in the neck of the bottle, a vulcanized india-rubber tube *h* is inserted in the cylindrical portion of the stopper, between two hemispherical portions *g*. In a modification, the stopper consists of three glass spheres formed in one piece, the middle sphere being covered with india-rubber. In another stopper, two unequal glass hemispheres are connected by a cylindrical portion, round which is placed an india-rubber tube. Instead of placing a tube around the cylindrical portion, an india-rubber cap is placed over each hemisphere, and the flange of each cap is shrunk over on to the ends of the cylindrical portion. In external stoppers for aërated liquids which are caused to evolve gas shortly after bottling, a projection for engaging with corresponding slots or grooves formed in the mouth of the bottle is cast or moulded on opposite sides of the plug of the stopper, so that the stopper is secured after insertion by turning it.

The stopper may be provided with a hole through the top, and with an india-rubber valve at the bottom. A glass or metal screw stopper is formed with a hole closed at the base by an india-rubber clack valve. A two-way tap and pipe are provided for filling, so that, when filling, the air may be allowed to escape. The valve is raised by pushing a stem or pin fitted in the hole.

1876

24. Sutcliffe, T., and **Fewings, J.** Jan. 3.

Bottling.—In turn-over machines for filling internally-stoppered bottles with aërated or other liquids, the bottles J, J^1, J^2, J^3 are held on the arms of a wheel C, with their mouths against a central nozzle D, by plates L, which are pressed towards the centre by spiral springs in the cylinders F, F^1, F^2, F^3, and they are tightened against the nozzle during the filling operation by levers H. The nozzle D has eight passages communicating with a four-way cock E at the back, four of the passages being for the admission of the liquid, and the other four for the escape of air. In connection with the air passages is a valve, arranged with a spiral spring regulated to the pressure required for filling. The nozzle has four hollow bosses, in which leather or india-rubber rings are secured by screw caps M. The syrup pump G is operated by tappets on the arms of the wheel, to draw in syrup just as the bottle arrives into the filling position J^2, and a spring at the bottom of the pump suddenly draws down the plunger at the moment the tappet passes the lever, and thus ejects the syrup through the passages into the bottle with the

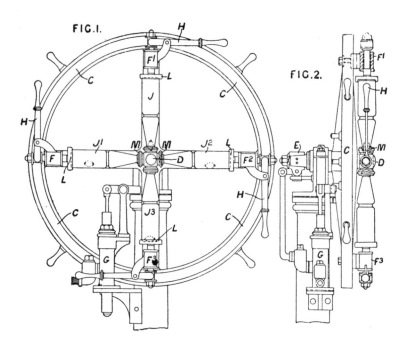

FIG.1.

FIG.2.

liquid. The pump may be worked by a hand-lever, in which case the syrup is forced through the cock into the bottle when in the position J^1.

Stoppers.—An oval or egg-shaped stopper a, Fig. 3, of glass, pottery, or other suitable material, is made of such size that it will just pass through the neck, and it is afterwards covered with an india-rubber envelope b by means of tongs or a split tube passed into the bottle. In another form, Fig. 4, a bell-shaped piece c of tin or other metal is cut out in grooves or spaces d, to allow the stopper to be compressed by the fingers; it has a solid metal head e, and the body is covered with india-rubber or other elastic material f. Stoppers of the form shown in Figs. 5 and 6 may also be used.

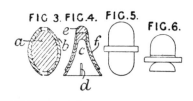

FIG 3. FIG.4. FIG.5. FIG.6.

---

307.   Lewis, J.   Jan. 26.

FIG.2.

Stoppers.—A stopper for a bottle containing aërated beverages is made of vulcanite, wood, glass, or other material, and of the shape shown in Fig. 2, or in the form of two truncated cones joined at their bases. An india-rubber or other washer is inserted in a deep groove in the stopper, and is held against the neck of the bottle by the internal pressure.

473. Barrie, P., and Samson, W. Feb. 5.

FIG.3.   FIG.5.

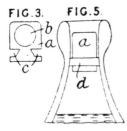

Stoppers for internally-stoppered aërated water bottles are made of lignum-vitae or other hard wood or metal, in the form of hollow cases containing pieces *b*, Fig. 3, of cork &c., in order to make them float perpendicularly in the liquid. When made of vulcanite or gutta-percha, the stopper is hollow and contains air. A groove *c*, towards the lower end of the cylindrical body *a* of the stopper, receives an india-rubber ring *d*, Fig. 5, or washer, which is pressed against the neck of the bottle by the internal pressure, when the stopper is in place. The bottle would also be sealed if, by accident, the stopper became inverted when the bottle was being filled. The end of the stopper does not project above the top of the neck when the bottle is filled with liquid, so that the packing of the bottles is facilitated. To insert the stopper, the washer is drawn out at one end until level with the outer surface of the stopper at the other, and is then twisted and lapped over the end of the stopper; after insertion into the bottle, the washer regains its correct position in the groove.

734. Claxton, C., and Claxton, C. Feb. 22.

FIG 2

Stoppers for aërated water &c bottles are formed with a spindle 1, which is slightly longer than the neck 2 of the bottle, and with a semi-circular head 3, which is pressed upon when the bottle is to be emptied. Three or more vanes or guides 4, for maintaining the stopper in the central position, and for guiding the liquid to the part of the mouth of the bottle not covered by the head 3, are formed on the spindle 1. An india-rubber washer 7, held between two flanges 5 and 6 on the spindle 1, is forced against the neck 2 by the internal pressure, to form an airtight joint, and is then prevented from doubling back by the larger flange 6. When the stopper is first inserted, the washer doubles upwards over the smaller flange 5, until the stopper is in position, and then springs into its groove. The liquid, when the stopper is forced inwards slightly, and the bottle is turned over, flows past the head 3. The stopper is preferably made of a mixture of spelter and tin, and is then unaffected by the contents of the bottle.

1589. Hannan, J. April 13.

Stoppers.—The neck *a* of a bottle for containing aërated liquids is screwed externally to receive a glass or porcelain cap *b*, by means of which the tubular india-rubber washer *d* is held in its place in a recess in the inside of the neck. The conical, spherical, or other internal stopper *f* is first inserted into the bottle, and is afterwards prevented from escaping by the washer *d*. The cap *b* may be further secured by

FIG.I.

means of a suitable adhesive material, which may also be employed without the use of the screw thread. According to the Provisional Specification, an outer band may also be secured round the connection between the cap and the bottle, in order to secure the stopper in its place.

1797. Walker, S. April 28.

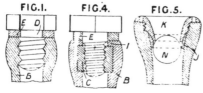
FIG.I.   FIG.4.   FIG.5.

Stoppers.—Relates to tapered and other screw stoppers, and to ball stoppers for aërated-water bottles. Fig. 1 shows a tapered screw stopper, in which is formed a recess D for receiving an india-rubber washer E. The stopper may be formed with parallel sides, and the groove D is then unnecessary. Fig. 4 shows a bottle neck B having an internal recess for receiving an india-rubber or other ring C, into which a taper stopper screws. The stopper is formed with a cylindrical neck which carries a washer E. The neck may be formed without the overhanging ledge I, a screw of coarser pitch being then employed.

In the aërated-water bottle shown in Fig. 5, a ball N presses against a rubber ring J held in place by a metal cap K which screws into the bottle neck. Holes O are formed in the cap K to receive a key. In a bottle with a parallel neck, a rubber ring is placed in the lower part of the screw-thread which receives the metal cap, and is pressed down by the cap.

2193. Codd, H. May 24.

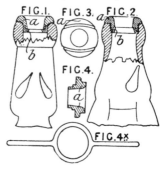
FIG.I.   FIG.3.   FIG.2.
FIG.4.
FIG.4x

Bottle necks.—Relates to bottles described in previous Specifications of the Applicant (No. 3070, A.D. 1870, and No. 4268, A.D. 1873), for containing aërated liquids, and closed by glass stoppers held against an elastic ring in the neck by the pressure within the bottle. In one arrangement, a loose glass cap *a*, Fig. 1, is inserted in the mouth of an ordinary bottle, and has a ring *b* of vulcanized india-rubber sprung upon it, the ring resting against a shoulder formed on the cap, and projecting below the cap. The cap is secured by wires passing over grooves in the cap *a*, Fig. 3, or by the wire or sheet metal fastening shown in Fig. 4 to pass over a flange on the stopper *a*, Fig. 4. The bottle neck is formed with contractions, as described in a previous Specification (No. 2621, A.D. 1872). In another arrangement, the ring *b*, Fig. 2, rests upon a shoulder in the bottle neck, and is held down by the cap *a*, the lower portion of which is formed as shown, to give a conical form to the ring; or the bottom of the cap may be flat. The caps are formed by pressing glass into moulds.

2714. Rule, T. July 1.

FIG.2.

Stoppers.—An internal stopper for a bottle for containing aërated liquid consists of a heavy core *a*, preferably dumb-bell-shaped, which is embedded in soft india-rubber.

2773. Rose, L. July 7.
[*Provisional protection only.*].

Bottles; stoppers.—Relates to stoppers for bottles for containing lemonade, soda, potash, or other aërated water, and to methods of retaining the stopper while pouring. A recess for retaining the stopper is formed at the middle or bottom of a bottle, and the bottom has a conical projection which throws the stopper into the recess when it falls. In a bottle for aërated liquids of low pressure, such as lemonade and other syrup drinks, the neck is elongated internally past the shoulder of the bottle, and thus forms a recess for retaining the stopper. In both forms of bottle, a ledge is made as a seat for the stopper in the neck of the bottle. An indented ring is formed on the outside of the neck, just below the mouth, in order to give a hold for a capsule. The stopper is in the form of two cones placed base to base with

heads at the ends of the cones. The cone portion is formed with several indented rings, and the heads or ends have V-shaped recesses. An india-rubber tube is drawn over the stopper, and the grooves enable it to be inserted in the bottle ready for use. A stopper may be formed with recessed ends and indented ring.

4339. Breffit, E., and Edwards, J. Nov. 9.

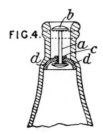

FIG.4.

Stoppers.—In a stopper for the bottles containing aërated liquids, a short stem *a* has a disc *b* at each end. A flexible india-rubber disc *d* fits loosely upon the stem, or may be fastened to an eyelet *c* which slides on the stem. The stopper is pushed down through the neck of the bottle, the disc being gathered round the stem during the passage. After passing through the neck, the disc assumes its original form, and is pressed by the gas from the liquid against a seat on the bottom of the neck.

4915. Lyon, J., Lyon, T., and Lyon, E. Dec. 20.

Stoppers.—In a stopper for bottles containing aërated liquids, a cylindrical plug A has a broad shallow recess B on one side of the centre, making one end heavier than the other. The plug is of earthenware, nickel, plated metal, or other heavy incorrodible material. At the lighter end a large india-rubber washer C is secured by a disc D, which will pass through the neck of the bottle. The disc is of tin or other metal which is unaffected by the liquids used.

FIG.5.

Many of the inventions patented between 1877 and 1883 were concerned with quicker, simpler, and/or less expensive methods of manufacturing stoppers for those bottles already on the market and selling in large numbers. Others suggested minor modifications to the shapes of existing internal stoppers and bottles.

Of the new inventors who appeared on the scene during this period the most noteworthy are Sykes & Macvay with their first attempt at an efficient internal closure; and Dan Rylands, whose first idea was patented in March 1882 at a time when he was in partnership with Hiram Codd at Barnsley. It was interference by Dan Rylands in the side of the business which Codd regarded as his prerogative that eventually resulted in the dissolution of the partnership in 1884. However, a compromise seems to have been reached in July, 1882 when both men co-operated on a patent which included the first attempt to make a Valve Codd. Rylands alone further improved on this idea in a specification dated November, 1883, though it was several years before he perfected the Rylands' Crystal Valve.

Note also the patent (British) for the American Hutchinson stopper by W. R. Lake in April, 1883. It achieved little success in this country in spite of its wide use in the United States.

1877

738. Macvay, W. W., and **Sykes, R.** Feb. 22. *Amended.*

FIG.5.

Stoppers.—The neck A of a bottle is formed with an internal thread having a shoulder a at the lower end, on which rests a rubber or like washer b forming the seat for a ball. The washer is pressed on the ball by means of a screwed glass, metal, wood, or other ferrule or cap c, having a milled edge or holes e for receiving a turning key. A metal washer may be placed between the washer b and cap.

960. Rose, L. March 9.

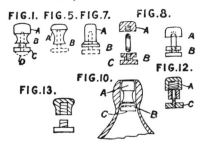

FIG.I. FIG.5. FIG.7. FIG.8.

FIG.IO.

FIG.I3.

FIG.I2.

Stoppers.—An internal stopper is made of china, earthenware, glass, bone, ivory, metal, heavy wood &c., with a rubber washer and a bottom of comparatively light material, such as cork, horn, vulcanite, non-porous wood &c. The cork or other light material serves as a float so that the stopper enters the neck in the right position when the liquid is bottled. When metal is used to weight the body of a stopper of wood, vulcanite, &c., the metal is covered so as not to come in contact with the liquid. Fig. 1 shows a stopper having the body A grooved at B for the rubber washer, and having a plug D of light material attached to the bottom C. Figs. 5 and 7 show other similar forms. Fig. 8 shows the parts A, C connected by a screw b. Figs. 12 and 13 show other forms built up of two or more parts. Fig. 10 shows a stopper in position in the bottle.

2952. Breffit, E., and Edwards, J. Aug. 1.

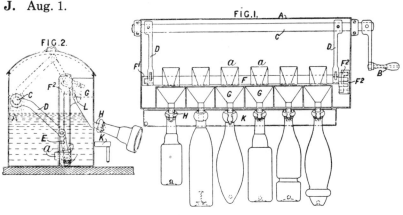

FIG.I.

FIG.2.

Bottling.—Relates to apparatus in which a number of measures are filled with liquid and discharged through funnels. The measures a, Figs. 1 and 2, are mounted on a bar F, which is attached by links E to crank-arms D on a shaft C which is operated by a handle B. The measures are alternately dipped into the liquid in the cistern A, and discharged into funnels G, having nozzles H which enter the bottles. One end of the bar F moves in a simple groove F^1, while the other moves in a compound groove F^2. The groove F^2, and toothed stop-pieces with which a toothed quadrant tilting-piece L engages, cause the containers to discharge into the funnels. The drip and overflow are caught by a trough K. The cistern A may be supplied by a ball valve, and

31

may be partitioned, so that different liquids can be simultaneously bottled by the same machine. The rock-shaft C may carry measures on both sides, thus rendering the apparatus double-acting. Measures of different sizes may be employed, or displacing-blocks may be placed in the measures.

Note. Although the above does not refer to a closure, the illustration is included to show the range of bottles Breffit & Edwards expected to handle on their filling machine in 1877.

3753. Pitt, S., [*Hicks, W.*]. Oct. 9.

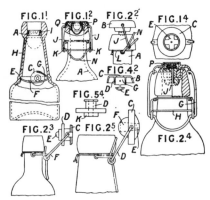

Stoppers.—Relates to closing-devices for bottles containing aërated or gaseous liquids. A bottle to be closed by internal pressure has an internal projection I, Fig. 1¹, over which is fitted a grooved elastic seat A to receive the glass or wooden stopper C. The lower part of the neck has a groove E to receive an elliptical bridge F, which prevents the stopper from falling into the bottle,

and has a claw G on one side to retain the stopper while the liquid is poured out. The bottle has a mark H opposite the claw to indicate the position in which the bottle is to be held while being emptied. In the closing-device shown in Figs. 1² and 2², the bottle A has a shoulder, and is fitted with a cap B, Fig. 4², having an opening C and a flange D provided with a support E for the stopper when moved from its seat. The stopper is contained within the chamber G, and is pressed against an annular compressible valve seat P, a grooved packing-piece Q surrounding the flange D to make a tight joint with the bottle neck. The flange is perforated to admit the pressure to the packing-ring. The cap is held in position by a bail wire J jointed to the cap and formed with journals K and a central part J to fit the bottle. A lever wire N has eyes to receive the journals K, and is pivoted in bearings formed in a wire L which surrounds the bottle neck beneath the shoulder. A stopper through which the bottle is filled with liquid under pressure consists of a cap C, Fig. 2³, held down by the wire mechanism F, and provided with a flexible packing-piece D having a perforated teat E through which the liquid is forced. The perforation is kept closed by the internal pressure acting against the convex surface of the teat. With the closing-device shown in Figs. 1⁴ and 2⁴, the bottle is filled without removing the cap. A double flanged packing-piece D, Fig. 5⁴, is inserted in the cap C which is held down by means of the lever wire G, and the controlling-wire H. The projection K forms a valve seat, and is strengthened by a band, the valve J having a conical-shaped upper surface to fit the seat, and being held in position by the internal pressure, and by a spring P placed round the spindle and pressing against an upper notched plate E secured to the valve stem. The valve is depressed from its seat during the filling operation. The bottle is opened by depressing the curved parts of the wires G, H away from the bottle, and is held clear of the bottle by pressing the curved part G against the neck.

3903. Codd, H. Oct. 22.

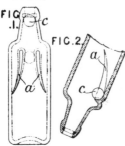

Bottles; stoppers.—In order to retain the internal stopper of a bottle containing an aërated liquid out of the neck when pouring, the bottle is formed with two convergent ridges *a*, Figs. 1 and 2, between which the spherical stopper *c* is held, instead of the ridges on the neck described in Specification No. 2621, A.D. 1872. The stopper *c* rests against an india-rubber washer when the bottle is closed, but falls to the bottom of the bottle when forced inwards, and is then caught between the ridges *a* when the bottle is tilted for pouring. The ridges at the upper ends may be raised so that the centre of the stopper lies below their upper edges when caught between them, and the bottle may then be completely inverted without the stopper being released. The bottle is blown in a mould which has internal projections corresponding with the desired ridges *a*. Two pairs of ridges may be

provided on each bottle. Internal stoppers, other than glass spheres, such as a glass cylinder carrying a washer ring of vulcanized india-rubber which bears against a shoulder round the neck of the bottle when the stopper is in place, may be used.

4660. Breffit, E., and Edwards, J. Dec. 8.

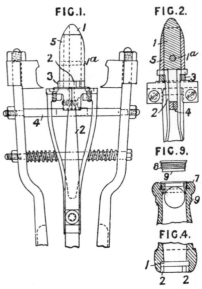

Bottle &c. necks, making.—The mouths or necks of glass bottles, jars, and other receptacles are constructed according to methods similar to those described in Specifications No. 4114, A.D. 1873, and No. 1616, A.D. 1875. The neck-forming tool has a plug 1, Figs. 1 and 2, formed in three parts, the main or body part being split axially and enclosed by a socket 5 secured by a pin 1. On inserting the plug into the neck of the vessel and closing the tongs, wedges 4 open the dogs 2, which protrude through openings in the socket 5 and form an annular

33

groove 1, Fig. 4, in the neck, or otherwise shape it when the tool is turned. Three or other number of radial projections on a loose collar 3, Figs. 1 and 2, on the plug form grooves 2, Fig. 4, passing from the end of the neck into the annular groove 1. The collar 3 may be serrated, grooved, or fluted to mould the neck so that it may receive plastic material for use in conjunction with external stoppers. The wedges 4 are shaped to act fully before the tongs are fully closed. In another method, suitable for fixing or embedding a metal ring in the necks of the reservoirs of oil lamps, siphon bottles, &c., the plug 1 carries a loose ring 7, Fig. 9, which is embedded in the bottle neck by pressing over the glass. The ring may be threaded to receive a flanged ring 8 carrying a rubber washer 9 to form a seat for an internal stopper. Other forms of necks are shown in Fig. 8.

FIG. 8

1878

164. Edmonds, G., and Edmonds, E. Jan. 12.

FIG.I. FIG.IO. FIG.7.

Stoppers.—Relates to internal stoppers of the type which are constructed with two or three bulbous parts, and a cap or tube of vulcanized india-rubber. Such stoppers are made with hollow bodies of sheet metal, preferably

Britannia metal. Fig. 1 shows a stopper with three bulbous parts *a*, *b*, *c* and a rubber tube *d* covering the part *b* and portions of the parts *a, c*. This stopper is made from the pair of blanks *g, f* shown in Fig. 7; each of these is produced from a thin disc which, by a drawing-through process, is made into a cup form and then into the form of a short tube with one end closed and hemispherical, a neck or contracted part being then made near the open end, by spinning. The open end of the blank *g* is then fitted on that of the blank *f*, and, by spinning or burnishing, or pressing in dies, the parts are closed together, to form the bulbous part *b*, Fig. 1, for the reception of the ring *d*. Fig. 10 shows a stopper having two bulbous parts *i, k* and a rubber cap *l*. The lower part *i* is made like the part *f*, Fig. 7, while the part *k* is a short cup-shaped piece, which is closed upon it by spinning &c. For bottles fitted with rubber rings in their necks, the stoppers may be used without the tube or cap.

874. Wharldale, W. March 4.

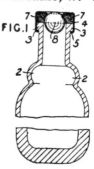

Stoppers; bottles.—A glass bottle for containing an aërated or a gaseous liquid, is made with a groove 2, Fig. 1, for retaining the stopper 8 during pouring. The ball or stopper 8 is forced by the gases inside the bottle against the india-rubber washer 7, which is kept in position by the metal cap 4, the lower edge of which is bent under the rim 3 formed on the bottle neck.

1601. Mitchell, F. B. April 20.

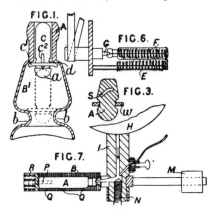

Stoppers.—In order to facilitate the washing, filling, and opening of internally-stoppered bottles containing aërated liquids, the bottles are made with cylindrical necks A, Fig. 1, surmounting conical or oval parts B^1 produced by forming depressions b^1 in the bottles. The stopper used consists of a cylindrical plug C of glass, earthenware, &c., which is formed with a double conical neck d immediately above the spherical lower end a. An india-rubber ring c^1 placed on the conical neck d is forced against the upper part of the chamber B^1 by the internal pressure, and the spherical head a is similarly forced against the ring c^1. When the stopper is pressed slightly, a groove c^2 in it passes below the ring c^1 and allows the gas to escape, thus releasing the stopper entirely. The stopper, in falling, is prevented by the ring c^1

from striking the bottle, and may be pushed aside to allow the brush used in cleaning the bottle to enter it. Fig. 3 shows an external stopper for bottles containing aërated liquids. A strong iron wire, which is bent and hinged at each side of the neck to another wire surrounding the neck, passes through the stopper A and rests in the upper horizontal part of a slot S in order to hold the stopper in position. The wire, while holding down the stopper, is inclined to the vertical axis of the neck so that the internal pressure tilts the stopper to one side slightly. When the stopper is pressed back in the opposite direction, the hinged wire slips into the inclined part of the slot S, thus freeing the stopper. When this form of stopper is used for bottles containing other than aërated liquids, the washer w rises above its groove. An internal stopper, which is turned to open the bottle consists of a plug as shown in Fig. 1 with an india-rubber washer at the bottom. When the stopper is turned by means of a lever inserted into a hole near its upper end, a notch in the rim of the washer comes under a raised portion or channel in the inside of the bottle immediately under the neck, and the gas then escapes and the stopper falls into the chamber B^1.

2771. Cherry, W. P., and Cherry, C. E. July 10.

Stoppers; stoppering.—A stopper for a bottle or similar vessel is made of wood, glass or other suitable material, and may be cylindrical, conical, spherical, or egg-shaped, so that it may be wedged tightly into a washer consisting of a tube of india-rubber placed inside the neck of the bottle. Rings of india-rubber may be inserted in grooves round the ends of the stopper, to prevent it from breaking the bottle when shaking about inside it. Figs. 2, 4, 8, 10, 11, and 15 show various forms of stopper A fixed in place in the

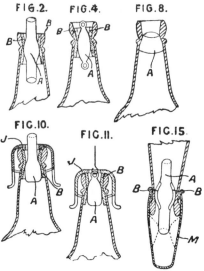

washer B. When the stopper is inserted from the outside, the washer B, Fig. 10, is placed over the smaller part of the stopper, with a metal ring J over it. The larger part of the stopper is placed in the neck of the bottle the ring J and washer B being then pressed down, and the stopper pulled upwards into position by means of pincers &c. In some cases, the stoppers are made with loops at the ends, so that a hook may be used for pulling them upwards. The bottle is afterwards opened by forcing the stopper into it, so that the washer can then be withdrawn by a hook. The washer may otherwise be attached to the stopper, and the stopper is then left in the bottle after opening it. In order to close the bottle with the stopper inside it, an india-rubber cap M, Fig. 15, is placed over the neck of the bottle, which is then inverted so that the stopper may be

gripped through the cap M and drawn into position. When the bottle contains an aërated liquid, the use of the cap M is dispensed with. When a plain cylindrical stopper is used, it is forced into position in the washer from the outside, a piece similar to the ring J, Fig. 10, but with a conical socket instead of a ring, being used to guide the stopper while it is being forced into the neck. The moulds used in casting glass and other stoppers are made with a number of holes, so that a number of stoppers may be cast at the one operation.

3111. Belleini, G. Aug. 7.

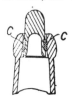

Stoppers.—A stopper for a bottle containing gaseous liquids consists of a hollow conical or bell-shaped plug of glass, wood, ebonite, earthenware, metal, &c., having a rubber or other elastic ring C fitted in a groove or recess. The larger end of the plug is in the bottle, the neck of which is tapered on the interior to correspond with the shape of the plug.

1879

725. Bull, W. Feb. 22.

Stoppers.—A bottle containing aërated or other liquids, and fitted with an internal or other stopper, is formed with a tapering or a contracted neck B, Fig. 1. The stopper A consists of two conical frusta joined together at their smaller ends, or formed in one piece and provided

36

with a sliding cork or similar collar *d*, so that, when the bottle is charged in the inverted position with an

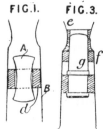

FIG.1.   FIG.3.

aërated liquid, the stopper is forced outwards and the collar is wedged between the stopper and the bottle neck. An ordinary cork *e*, Fig. 3, may be used when the bottle mouth is shaped as shown, and is then secured in position by a perforated soft-metal disc like a semi-capsule, by wire, or by forming a notch *f* in the mouth of the bottle.

893.   Breffit, E.   March 6.

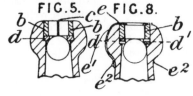

FIG.5.   FIG.8.

Stoppers.—Relates to methods of securing a seating for an internal stopper in a bottle mouth. The mouth of the bottle shown in Fig. 5 is conical internally, and is formed with a shoulder on which rests a flexible seating *d*. Two semi-cylindrical pieces *b* are placed above the seating *d*, and are held in place by driving in wood or other wedges *c*. The mouth of the bottle shown in Fig. 8 is cylindrical internally, and a glass or other ring *b*, placed above the ball seating, is held in place by a cap *e*, the arms e^1 of which are secured to the bottle by a wire e^2. An

india-rubber ring is placed between the cap *e* and the ring *b*. The ball seating consists of two cork rings *d*, arranged to break joint, and separated by an india-rubber washer d^1. This seating is intended for use with bottles containing liquids which would be injured by contact with india-rubber. If the bottle is perforated by means of the machine described in Specification No. 4660, A.D. 1877, the ring *b* may be riveted in the bottle mouth.

1210.   Vallet, L.   March 26.

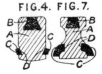

FIG.4. FIG.7.

Stoppers.—Internal stoppers for bottles containing aërated liquids are moulded from a mixture of about two parts of powdered or ground glass and one part of shellac, and then trimmed and polished. They may be strengthened by embedding or moulding wire, string, or other fibrous material within them. The head of the stopper may be weighted at B, or it may be made heavier by increasing the proportion of glass in it. The groove D for receiving the washer C may be formed with inclined sides, as shown in Fig. 4, or it may be shaped, as shown in Fig. 7, to receive a rubber tube C. The bottle neck is provided with a ledge to form a seat for the washer C.

1861.   Barrett, H,   May 10.

Stoppers.—Spherical or otherwise shaped internal stoppers and washers or stopper-seatings for bottles containing aërated liquids are made of vulcanized india-rubber or like materials, which become soft on heating them and harden on cooling. The stoppers may be moulded inside the bottles by tools c, Fig. 2,

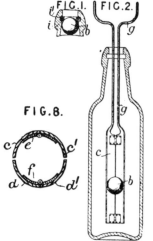

FIG.1. FIG.2.

FIG.8.

the ebonite, lionite, or like material for forming the ball *b* being passed into the bottle and pressed and rolled into shape by the tools. The diameter of the ball may be greater or less than the diameter of the bottle neck. Two tools, consisting of flaps *c, c¹, d, d¹*, Fig. 8, connected by hinges *e, f*, are passed into the bottle by handles *g*, Fig. 2. The tools are heated so as to soften the material, which may be passed in hot or cold. Similar tools may be made with three segments or flaps, two of which are hinged together. The ball may be made by inserting sufficient softened material and by revolving the bottle. A hollow or solid ball of hard vulcanite or ebonite, sufficiently large to form a stopper, may be softened and elongated by heating it, and passed into the bottle. On cooling, it regains its original shape. The stopper may be weighted by a shot to render it heavier than water. The seatings for the stoppers consist of soft rubber rings *i*, Fig. 1,

vulcanized to hard rubber rings i^1, which, when heated, may be passed into the grooves in the bottle necks, and, on cooling, prevent the seatings from coming out. The rings may also be fitted with outer soft rings, which accommodate themselves to irregularities in the grooves in the necks.

1966. Battersby, W. May 16.

FIG.3. FIG.5. FIG.6.

Stoppers.—Relates to internal stoppers which present a large surface of contact with the bottle, and are weighted in order to fall automatically into position in the bottle mouth. The stopper shown in Fig. 6 has a hard vulcanized head A and a soft base B, while the stopper shown in Fig. 3 is of homogeneous india-rubber, but a ball or weight is embedded in its head. The flexible neck of the latter stopper facilitates its insertion in the bottle. A glass, wood, or ebonite stopper, shown in Fig. 5, has a hollow hemispherical base, on which an india-rubber washer C is placed. Another stopper is double-ended and has a washer at the middle.

2628. Grimwade, E. W., [*Mount, L. le B.*]. June 30.

FIG.1.

Stoppers.—The necks of aërated-water bottles are constructed to receive an india-rubber, cork, or

38

other washer A made in the form of a hollow truncated cone, the lower edge of which rests on a ledge B formed in the neck. A spherical or other stopper having a circular horizontal section is placed into the bottle before the washer is applied, and when the bottle is filled, bears against the washer. In a modification, a projecting rim is formed on the washer round the lower edge, and fits into a recess formed in the neck.

3217. Kitching, H. Aug. 11.

FIG.2.

Stoppers.—For bottles containing aërated liquids, the stopper consists of a hollow conical-shaped plug *a* having an enlarged head *c*, and straight or concave sides, as shown. An elastic ring or washer *e* is placed round the plug after it has been dropped into the bottle. Projections and grooves on the bottle neck are thus dispensed with, bottles of ordinary construction being used.

3869. Codd, H. Sept 25.

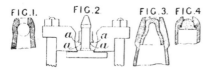

FIG.1.   FIG.2   FIG.3. FIG.4

Stoppers.—Relates to improvements on the mode of stoppering described in Specification No. 3070, A.D. 1870. A spherical seating is provided in the neck for the ball stopper, as shown in Fig. 1. The stopper may be of other forms, as shown in Fig. 3 and 4, the neck being in all cases provided with a seating of corresponding contour.

3935. Barrett, H. Sept. 30.

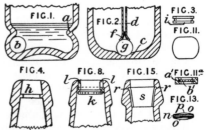

Bottles; stoppers; bottling; stoppering.—Relates to the construction of stoppers and seatings for internally-stoppered bottles for aërated liquids, beer, &c., and to means for bringing the stoppers to their seats when bottling, and for retaining them when pouring. Ball stoppers of glass, earthenware, or the like are made hollow so as to float or sink slowly. For those that sink, the bottom of the bottle is formed with an undercut projection *a*, Fig. 1, to retain the stopper *b* while pouring. Ball stoppers may be brought to their seats, when the bottles are filled, by means of a tube *d*, Fig. 2, open to the atmosphere or provided with a piston and having a rubber-lined funnel-shaped end *f*. The bottom of the bottle is formed with a central recess *c* to keep the stopper *g* central, and the stopper is brought to its seat by quickly withdrawing the tube *d*. A washer for ball stoppers is made of soft or combined soft and hard rubber, as described in Specification No. 1861, A.D. 1879, but with an annular groove *i*, Fig. 3, to fit over an internal flange *h*, Fig. 4, in the bottle neck. When floating stoppers are used in bottling beer and other malt liquors, the required pressure for keeping the

39

stopper against its seat is obtained by introducing a small quantity of compressed air into the bottle, or into the cask from which the beer is drawn. An internal stopper may be made of hard inelastic material, such as pearl, ivory, or glass, and in the form of a disc preferably slightly oval, as shown in Fig. 11. Grooves *l, l,* Fig. 8, are left in an internal shoulder in the bottle neck, to permit insertion or removal of the stopper *k* when the washer is not in place. The washer is also made of oval shape, and of a suitable hard material, such as ivory, bone, vulcanite, or glass, and with a thin ring of compressed cork cemented to each side. The washer is passed in edgewise through the grooves *l, l,* and is cemented in a recess with its larger diameter in line with the grooves. A washer of vulcanized rubber may be used instead of the compound washer. If the disc stopper *k* is made of heat-resisting material, the grooves *l, l,* may be dispensed with, the stopper being inserted before the neck is closed in.

1880

49. Grimwade, E. W., [*Felton, A.,* and *Grimwade, F. S.*]. Jan. 6.

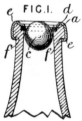

FIG.1.

Stoppers.—Bottles for containing aërated liquids are formed with an annular groove *a* in the top of the neck. An india-rubber or other elastic ring *d* is placed in the groove,

and is secured by a soft-metal cap *e,* which is turned round a shoulder *f* on the outside of the neck of the bottle. The bottle is closed by a ball or other shaped stopper *c,* which is forced by the gas from the liquid against the washer.

2488. Lamont, J. June 19.

FIG.4.   FIG.5.

Stoppers.—A glass or other internal stopper for bottles containing aërated or gaseous liquids, and specially intended for the bottles described in Specification No. 1923, A.D. 1874, is provided with a stem or body *a,* Fig. 5, preferably slightly conical and near the base is a groove for the reception of a rubber washer, ring, or tube *d.* The bottom of the stopper is recessed or hollow, as shown in Fig. 4, thus ensuring, from the weight of the head portion of the stopper, that the stopper always falls into its proper position in the neck of the bottle.

3709. Neal, J. Sept. 11.

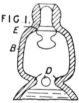

FIG.1.

Stoppers.—The neck B of a bottle for containing aërated liquids is blown or moulded with four interior projections D, which prevent the stopper from falling into the body of the bottle, and is made so large that the stopper does not obstruct the passage of the liquid or of a cleaning-brush, while the stopper cannot become inverted in the neck B. An india-rubber washer E is pressed into a groove in the stopper, and is forced against the neck of the bottle by the pressure of the gas, so that only a small surface is exposed to the action of the liquid.

3747. Codd, H. Sept. 15. [*Letters Patent void for want of Final Specification.*].

Bottle necks.—The opposite sides of the necks of bottles containing aërated liquors are indented so as to form in each bottle two inclined shelves, on which the opposite edges of the glass disc-like stopper come to rest as the stopper falls away from its seat. The inclines are continued diagonally across the neck, which may be contracted and corrugated so that the disc cannot fall into the bottle. The neck may be made with a double passage, in one part of which the stopper lodges, while the liquor may be poured out through the other part. Reference is made to a method of forming bottle necks with internal projections for retaining ball stoppers described in Specification No. 2621, A.D. 1872.

5264. Trotman, F. Dec. 15.

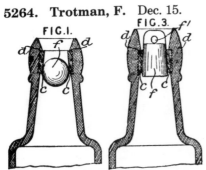

Stoppers.—The neck of a bottle for aërated liquids is formed with a recess *d* in which a cork liner *c* is placed. A ball or plug stopper *f* tightens up against the liner when the bottle is charged. In the case of the plug, it may be pierced with a hole f^1 for a hook or other device for lifting the plug into position. When the stopper is pressed away, it falls away from the neck, which is not formed with a contracted portion.

1881

1125. Codd. H. March 15.

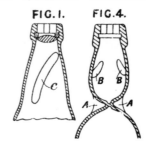

Bottle necks.—Relates to bottles for aërated liquids stoppered with internal glass stoppers of a disc-like form, and to means for preventing the disc from falling to the bottom of the bottle and for guiding it back to its seat when the bottle is refilled and inverted. The opposite sides of the neck of the bottle are indented so as to form two inclined shelves C, Fig. 1, formed so that the disc slides down to and remains at a part of the neck which is of sufficient diameter for the liquid to pass freely as it is poured out. The inclines do not allow room for the disc in any position to turn over or set itself on edge; it can only slide and pass along the inclines to and from its seat. The neck may be contracted and corrugated a short distance below the disc, which then cannot fall past the contraction and lodges with its edges in the corrugations; or the neck may be made with two or more separate passages by pinching it in by conical points at A, A, Fig. 4, so that the disc guided by internal ridges B, B lodges in one passage and the liquid can pass through the other or others. The disc stopper is inserted edgewise through grooves inside the head as described in Specification No. 3835, A.D. 1879. Contracted necks for retaining ball stoppers as described in Specification No. 2621, A.D. 1872, are referred to.

2338. Davidson, J. S. May 27.

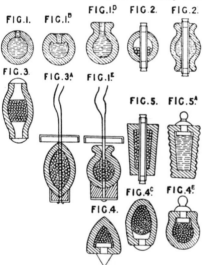

Stoppers for bottles or other vessels containing aërated, gaseous, or other liquids, such as beer, wine, oil, &c., are formed of cases or bags of elastic or waterproof material, filled or partly filled with solid or liquid substance. The cases or bags may be of spherical, conical, oval, or other shape, and they may be used with bottles having necks of any shape. They may have one opening as shown in Figs. 1, 1^B, 1^D, or two openings, as shown in Figs, 2, 2^A,

and 3 which are closed by plugs or by a tube fitted with a ball, plug, or cork. This ball, plug, or cork may be used for relieving the pressure when the stoppers are used for aërated waters, or for enabling a portion of the liquid to be withdrawn. If the stopper is to be internal, the case is passed into the bottle neck and is then filled or partly filled with the substance, either sand, gravel, &c., or water, by means of a funnel-shaped instrument; when it is expanded to the form of, but slightly larger than, the neck, the instrument is drawn out, and the opening is closed by its own elasticity or by a spring, wire, or plug. If the bottle contains non-aërated liquid, the stopper has attached to it a string or wire by which it is pulled up into the neck, as shown in Figs. 3 and 1 . If the bottle neck tapers gradually larger to the mouth, the stopper is inserted from the outside after the manner of a cork, and forms an external stopper; the case is shaped accordingly and may have either a plain or ribbed or corrugated surface, as shown in Figs. 5 and 5 . The stopper may have top and bottom buttons drawn together by a wire &c. to cause it to be pressed against the bottle neck. Figs. 4, 4 , and 4 show other forms of stoppers fitted with closing plugs or buttons.

3102. King, A. T. July 16.

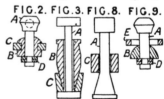

Stoppers.—A stopper for bottles for containing aërated or other liquids consists of a central plunger of wood, ivory, porcelain, ebonite, earthenware, or glass &c., and an india-rubber washer which is expanded otherwise pressed against the interior of the neck of the bottle. In the form shown in Fig. 2, the plunger A slides through a body B, which is grooved to receive a washer C. The washer C may be in the form of a frustum of a cone, enveloping the body B and having an internal flange entering the groove in the body B. The plunger A is also formed with a neck above its lower head for the reception of one or two washers D. In opening a bottle, the spindle A is first depressed to permit the escape of gas between the spindle and the body B. A simplified form of this stopper consists of a plunger passing through an india-rubber washer and having a head at each end. In a stopper suitable for a bottle for containing still liquids, a washer C, Fig. 3, is expanded by forcing downwards a body B which has a conical end. In another stopper for the same purposes, shown in Fig. 8, the lower end of the plunger A is conical, and, after the washer C has been pushed past the smallest part of the bottle neck, the plunger is pulled upwards in order to expand the washer. Fig. 9 shows a stopper suitable for a bottle having an internal flange in its mouth. A loose washer E is expanded against the neck and internal flange of the bottle by an india-rubber or other hemispherical body B.

4646. Warner, C. M. Oct. 24.

Stoppers; bottles.—A bottle for aërated or gaseous liquids, which is closed by a glass or other ball D, Fig. 2, is screwed inside the neck and fitted with a plug B, preferably of tin, white metal, or porcelain. This plug covers the top of the bottle neck,

and may extend for a short distance down the outside of the neck, as shown, and carries, in a groove, a ring E of india-rubber, and below this, a ring of cork F, which is held in position by the turned-up portions B[4] of the plug, and which prevents the contents from coming in contact

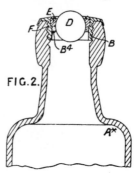

FIG. 2.

with the rubber ring. When the bottle is closed, the ball D projects slightly above the plug B, and leaves no space for the accumulation of dust &c. The bottle is made with a rectangular or nearly rectangular annular shoulder A , which retains the stopper while the contents are being drawn off.

1882

1486. Rylands, D. March 28.

Bottle necks, making; stoppers.— The recesses for holding the washers of internally-stoppered bottles are made with a dovetailed section, so that the sides of the recesses or grooves grip the washers, which are inserted by a special tool. The dovetail-shaped dogs b, Fig. 2, are mounted upon a spring a attached to a stem c^1, and are pressed outwards through slots in the plug c by a stem g, which is moved up or down by the quadrants g^1. The exterior of the neck f is formed by dies f^1, and the dogs b are rotated by the disc d, which carries the plug c and is carried by a fork k attached to the stem c^1. When the workman releases the bows h, they spring open, and the quadrants fall, the studs l sliding

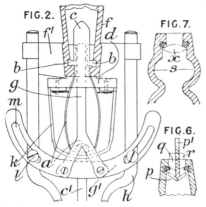

in the slots m, and the stem g allows the springs a to remove the dogs b from the groove they have formed. The dogs may be grooved so as to corrugate the sides of the recess. Fig. 6 shows the instrument for inserting the washers. A screwed stem p^1 is fitted with two flaps p and a plug q, which is held in place by a nut r. The washer is placed over the flaps p, and is pressed into the neck by the plug q; the flaps fall into the position shown, and enable the workman to press the washer into the groove. The screw r is then drawn back so that the stem may be pushed into the bottle, which is then inverted, so that the flaps fall against the stem, and may be withdrawn through the washer.

Bottles.—In bottles for aërated liquids, a bulb s, Fig. 7, is formed in the neck to facilitate the fall of the disc stopper x into position, and to hold the stopper when pouring out the contents or while washing the bottle.

1898. Ballard, J. April 21.

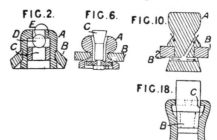

Stoppers.—Relates to stoppers for bottles containing aërated and fermented liquids. One form of stopper consists of a perforated stud A, Fig. 2, fitted with a rubber washer B and a rubber sphere or disc D, which, when the spring E is depressed, allows the gas to escape, when the stopper falls to the bottom of the bottle. The sphere or disc is kept in position by a wood ferrule C. The disc D may be fixed to a push-button C, Fig. 6, and pressed against the underside of the stud A by means of a silvered or galvanized spring. In the case of the stopper shown in Fig. 10, the gas is allowed to escape by depressing a stud A, thus opening the ends of the hold B^2, or the inclined passages in the stopper may be replaced by holes through the washer B, the stud A then being rotated to bring the ends of the passage B^2 into coincidence with the holes in the washer. The stoppers, when made of wood, are weighted with block tin at their upper ends. Stoppers of the second kind are provided with cork or other ferrules B, Fig. 18., and projections C which are passed through notches in the bottle necks. To fix the stoppers, they are slightly rotated. The projections C may be above or below the washer B, or may engage with rims on the outside of the bottle necks.

1992. Burdin, I. April 27.

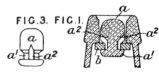

FIG.3. FIG.I.

Stoppers.—An internal stopper *a*, Figs. 1 and 3, is formed with vertical or inclined venting-grooves a^1, so that, when the stopper is depressed, the pressure in the bottle is relieved. The washer *b* is placed on the neck a^1 of the stopper, and is forced against an internal ridge in the bottle mouth by the gas pressure.

3041. Froggatt, W. June 28.

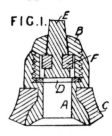

FIG.I.

Stoppers.—The body of an internal stopper for bottles is grooved to receive a rubber washer C, Fig. 1, and may be in two parts A, B screwed together, or in one part, the piston E then being prevented from falling down through the part A by means of a ferrule screwed into the lower end of the part A; or, the piston may be tapered in the direction opposite to that shown. To open the bottle, the washer F carried by the piston E is pushed down from its seat and against the ferrule or rubber ring D, thus allowing the air or gases to escape, and then preventing the overflow of the aërated liquid. A small pressure on the piston E then causes the stopper to fall.

3252. Codd, H., and Rylands, D. July 8.

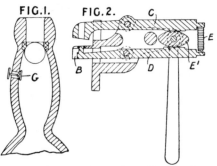

FIG.I. FIG.2.

Bottle necks; bottle necks, making.—To facilitate the opening of internally-stoppered bottles, a small hole is made in the neck, and fitted with an inwardly-opening valve G, by which the gas can be withdrawn to free the stopper. The hole is formed, by means of a punch, shown in Fig. 2, while the bottle is still hot after its removal from the mould. The neck is placed upon the plate B, and the levers C, D are forced together by means of a cam E^1 operated by a hand-lever E, so that the punch is driven through the neck. The hole may be drilled by a sand blast in old bottles.

3257. King, A. T. July 10.

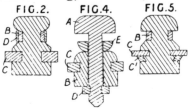

FIG.2. FIG.4. FIG.5.

Stoppers.—An internal stopper for a bottle containing aërated liquid is weighted by a strip B, Fig. 2, of lead, tin, lead coated with tin, alloy, or other suitable material clamped into a groove in the stopper. The strip B may be covered by a rubber band D. A washer C for making the joint is placed in another groove in the stopper, or two thin washers C, C^1, Fig. 5, may be used. In a stopper provided, as shown in Fig. 4, with a plunger A, which, when pressed down, allows the gas to escape, a weighting-ring E is placed round the plunger before it is inserted in the stopper, and a washer D is placed in a groove in the plunger after it has been inserted. The plunger and the stopper may be grooved, to allow the gas to escape more readily.

3417. Cook, J. C. July 18.

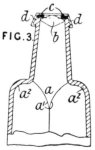

FIG.3.

Stoppers.—A glass or earthenware stopper b, Fig. 3, for a mineral-water bottle is made with curved or angular faces, and is forced upwards against the rubber ring c, which is kept in position by means of the spun metal cap d.

Bottles.—A mineral-water bottle is made of a flattish oval shape just below the neck, to retain the stopper while pouring, each side a, Fig. 3, being pressed inwards to form curved or heart-shaped surfaces a^1 outside and chambers a^2 inside. The bottom of the bottle may be flat or conical.

4347. Wild, A. J. T. Sept. 12.

Stoppers; bottle necks.—Stoppers for bottles for containing aërated or other liquids are so constructed that the liquid does not come in contact with the washer. In the stopper shown in Figs. 1 and 1a, the head c carries a shank c^4, at the end of which are formed projections c^3 which take under ribs a in the mouth

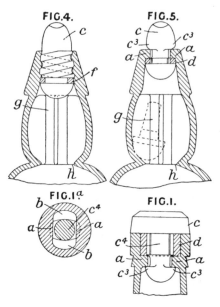

FIG.4.   FIG.5.

FIG.1^a.   FIG.1.

of the bottle. A cork washer d is placed on the shank c^4. Figs. 4 and 5 show stoppers which fall into the bottle, when the bottle is opened. The stopper c, Fig. 4, screws into the mouth of the bottle, and forces the washer f against the sides of the conical mouth. The stopper may be held in place by a bayonet-joint, as shown in Fig. 5, projections c^3 on the shank engaging with ledges a at the bottle mouth. The head of the stopper may be formed with a recess for a stopper key. In order to retain the stopper while pouring, the neck of the bottle is constricted at h, and two internal ridges g are formed at opposite sides of the neck.

4565. Pullan, A. Sept. 25.

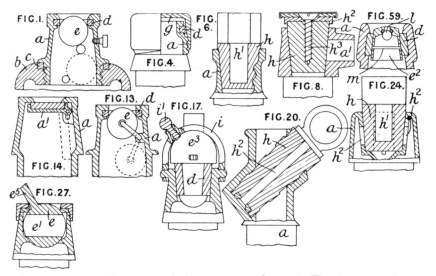

Stoppers; corks, retaining; bottles.—Relates to internal and other stoppers for bottles, and to methods of retaining stoppers while pouring. In order to permit the insertion of an internal stopper *e*, Fig. 1, the neck *a* of the bottle is removable, and screws into the body *b*. The joint is rendered tight by a washer *c* of vulcanized fibre, paper, or parchment &c., and a washer *d* is let into the neck to form a seating for the stopper *e*. The neck may be of glass, metal, ebonite, or vulcanized fibre &c. A cover *g*, Fig. 4, which screws on to the exterior of a bottle neck, is conical internally, and bears on a washer *d*. A stopper screwing into a bottle mouth has a conical neck, which bears on to a washer let into the bottle mouth. A cork *h*, Fig. 6, is formed with a partial or complete screw-thread, which engages with a screw-thread in the bottle mouth. The cork is strengthened by an internal metal plug h^1 projecting from a metal cap. In the arrange-ment shown in Fig. 8, an opening a^1 at the side of a bottle mouth may be closed by a cork *h*, which screws into the bottle mouth. A metal cap h^2 is attached to the cork by a screw h^3. A washer *d*, Fig. 59, may be let into the bottle mouth, and form a seating for a hollow conical metal stopper e^2, or a weighted conical cork may be forced by the gas pressure into a conical seating in a neck screwed into the body of the bottle. A hinged cover a^1, Fig. 14, may be arranged to open internally or externally, and be held by a catch or thum-screw. Fig. 13 shows a ball stopper *e* connected by a link to a projection in the bottle mouth. A stopper e^3, Fig. 17, having a hemispherical head and a washer *d*, may be held in place by a screw i^1 in a yoke *i*. In the arrangement shown in Fig. 20, a cork *h*, strengthened by an internal rod h^2, terminating in a ring to which a guard chain may be attached, is screwed horizontally or in an inclin-ed direction into a bottle mouth, so

47

that the pressure acts on the sides of the stopper. Fig. 24 shows a bottle mouth a so shaped that the gas pressure acts only on the sides of the cork h through apertures h^2. A ball e, Fig. 27, formed with a passage e^1, may be held in a seating in a bottle mouth in such a manner that it can be turned by means of a projection e^5, or by means of an instrument inserted in a recess in the stopper, so that the passage e^1 is brought into line with the bottle mouth.

1883

1770. Lake, W. R., [*Hutchinson, C. G.*]. April 7.

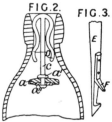

FIG.2. FIG.3.

Stoppers; stoppering.—Relates to an internal stopper for bottles containing aërated liquids &c. which is held in place by springs, and to a hook for drawing the stopper to its seat when the bottle has been filled. A shank c, Fig. 2, has two discs a^1, a^{11} preferably cast in one with it. The disc a^1 is smaller than the disc a^{11} and the washer a is drawn down the shank c and over the upper disc a^1. A bent spring D is then attached, preferably by soldering to the shank c. The spring D grips the interior of the neck and holds the stopper in place while pouring and when closed. The hook F, Fig. 3, of the bottling machine has an inclined projection F which guides the hook and if the stopper spring is not vertical strikes it and moves it over the hook. The

hook may be double in order to catch both loops of the spring. The Provisional Specification states also that the shank of the stopper may be bent to an 8 form with one end free, thus forming a spring in itself. The neck of the bottle is contracted somewhat below to prevent the passage of the upper and larger loop of the stopper. In removing the washer from a stopper the washer is gripped between the hook set in a handle and a bar sliding in the handle. The ends of the hook and bar are preferably spurred. In a bottling machine the bottle is placed on a disc carried by a rod connected to a treadle. The bottle is raised against a cushion at the end of a vertical cylinder. The bottle is filled by a pipe controlled by a cock, and a hook carried by a plunger working in the cylinder is then lowered and raised again in order to draw the stopper to its seat. The plunger is carried by a rod passing through a stuffing-box at the top of the cylinder and operated by a lever.

1957. Edwards, J. April 18.

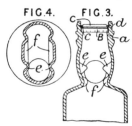

FIG.4. FIG.3.

Bottle necks; stoppers.—The neck of an internally-stoppered bottle is formed with a shoulder a, Fig. 3, for the washer B and also with a groove d to receive a spring-ring c, which bears against a cap C having a central hole, and fixes the washer in place. Internal projections e retain the stopper in position while pouring out the liquid. An inclined rib f, Fig. 4, at each side of the neck guides the stopper to the projections e when it is forced into the bottle.

2176. Sankey, R. J. April 30.

FIG. 2.

Stoppers.—The elastic seating d, Fig. 2, of an internal stopper for aërated water and similar bottles, is fixed in position by means of a vulcanite ring e. This ring is compressed so as to pass through the bottle mouth, and is then expanded by the application of heat. The shoulder b may be above the seating and ring, or two rings may be used, the interior of the neck being of an oval shape, or the rings may be expanded into or against notches or projections. The stopper c is of a double-conical shape, and is hollow.

2512. Vanes, A. B. May 19.

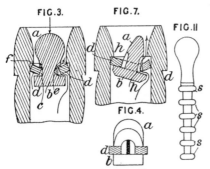
FIG. 3. FIG. 7. FIG. II FIG. 4.

Stoppers.—In internal stoppers, for bottles containing aërated liquids, the stopper body a, Fig. 3, is formed with a flange b, above which the body is contracted, as shown at c, and fitted with an india-rubber washer d. This washer is drawn up against a projection f in the bottle neck when in position. The neck c of the stopper is provided with a groove e, so that when the stopper is forced down to open the bottle, this groove affords a passage for the escape of gases from the bottle. The upper side of the flange may have a circular rib to assist the bedding of the washer. The groove e may be dispensed with by using a perforated washer, or by a washer which fits the neck c loosely. The upper part of the body may be pear-shaped, as shown in Fig. 3, or wedge-shaped, as in Fig. 4, or of a flattened cone-shape, as in Fig. 7. Vent holes h, Fig. 7, may be made on both sides of the contracted neck. The stoppers may be weighted to cause it to enter the mouth of the bottle in filling, by riveting a metal bar in the head of the stopper, or by plugging holes in the head with lead, the holes running in various ways, so that the weight cannot become detached. A gauge for indicating the size of a stopper required for a bottle consists of a rod or plate carrying a number of discs or spheres s, Fig. 11, progressively increasing in diameter from the lower end.

2599. Macvay, W. W., and **Sykes, R.** May 24.

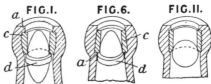
FIG. I. FIG. 6. FIG. II.

Stoppers.—The neck of an internally-stoppered bottle is formed at the upper end with an internal flange a, Fig. 1, and also with a bulge directly below the flange to receive the washer c, which is forced in place by a machine. In Fig. 6, the neck is tapered and the washer rests on a shoulder *a*, while in Fig. 11, the neck, below the flange, is formed with a screw-thread or serrations to hold the washer in place. The washer may be made of cork or other suitable material. When cork is used, it is rendered non-porous by steeping it in a chemical composition. The stopper is formed with a collar *d*, Figs. 1 and 6, to bear against the underside of the washer, and with conical ends or one conical end only; or it may be made spherical, as shown in Fig. 11.

2883. Sankey, R. J. June 9.

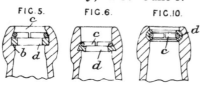

Stoppers.—Relates to improvements in the stoppers for internally-stoppered bottles containing aërated or gaseous liquids, described in Specification No. 2176, A.D. 1883, and consists in fixing the rubber rings or seatings by means of divided rings of vulcanite &c. which enables the washers to be readily removed and replaced. Fig. 5 shows a ring or washer *d* held on the shoulder *b* by a cut or divided ring *c*. In Fig. 6 the ring *d* is held in a groove in the neck by a cut ring *c*. Fig. 10 shows an arrangement in which a long rubber washer or seating *d* is held in a groove in the bottle neck by a cut ring *c* bearing against its central portion. The fixing-ring is contracted, placed in the neck, and allowed to expand into position. A fixing of metal may be placed in the neck and then expanded by a tool until it fits tightly against the washer or seating.

4863. Vallet, L. Oct. 12.

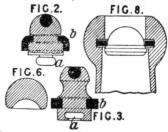

Stoppers.—Relates to the internal stoppers described in Specification No. 490, A.D. 1875, which are weighted to cause them to fall into position in the bottle mouth. To permit the removal of a stopper from a bottle without removing its washer *b* the base of the stopper is provided with a knob or recess *a* by which it can be grasped by pliers and drawn out of the bottle base upwards. The mouth of the bottle shown in Fig. 8 has a groove for the washer. The stopper, which is similar to the stopper shown in Fig. 6, has a hollowed base, so that, in bottling, the stopper falls head foremost. The shape of the stopper prevents it from rolling into the mouth of the bottle while pouring. The neck of the bottle is straight to facilitate cleaning.

5445. Rylands, D. Nov. 19.

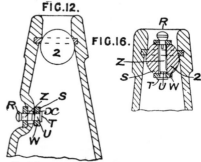

Bottle necks; stoppers; opening internally-stoppered bottles.— Refers to Specification No. 3525,

A.D. 1882. The valve hole in the bottle neck, instead of being formed after the bottle is removed from the mould, is formed while it is therein.

In another arrangement, the valve is applied to the marble 2, as shown in Fig. 16, instead of to the bottle neck. The hole is formed in the marble 2 during the process of pressing.

In the early months of 1884 the Codd-Rylands partnership came to its stormy end. For the next three years both inventors attempted to gain the lion's share of the internally-stoppered bottle market. Codd concentrated on perfecting tools to form bottle necks and grooves; his best effort with stoppers was a disc-shaped device patented in 1884-85. Dan Rylands' main concern was with his 'Valve' idea. He patented several improvements to it and further developed the various tools used in the bottle's manufacture.

By 1887 Hiram Codd was dead and Dan Rylands' Barnsley bottleworks was able to consolidate its position as the largest factory in the world devoted to the production of internally-stoppered mineral water bottles. More than seventy five per cent of all bottles supplied to soft drinks makers in Britain and the Empire were by 1888 being made by Dan Rylands.

Some of those manufacturers and inventors who shared the remaining twenty five per cent of the market—Lamont, Vallet, Barrett, Breffit, Sutcliffe and others—made slight improvements to their bottles during this period but there were no major developments until the widespread use of coloured glass after 1888.

1884

5826. Barrett, H. April 2.

Stoppers.—The bottom of stoppers made of glass or porcelain is provided with a disc or washer of ebonite or wood to make it lighter than the head, and at the same time to prevent chipping by striking against the bottle. The bottom may be screwed on, or fixed in various ways, and passages may be made to allow the escape of gas between the india-rubber washer and the stopper when the latter is pressed.

11,611. Sharpe, I. R. Aug. 25.

Stoppers.—The bottle neck is formed with two sets of internal projections. The lower set G prevents the ball-stopper E from falling into the body of the bottle. The upper set F consists of smaller

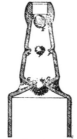

projections, and allows the ball to pass when the bottle is in a vertical position, but prevents it from closing the mouth when the liquid is being poured out. The projections are made by making indentations on the outside of the neck when in the process of manufacture.

12,453. Rylands, D. Sept. 16. [*Patent refused.*]

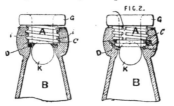

Stoppers; opening internally-stoppered bottles.—An internal thread C is made in the neck B of the bottle; at the bottom of the thread is a ledge on which rests an elastic washer D. A tubular externally-threaded stopper A with head G screws into the neck and presses against the washer D, making an airtight joint. The ball K is forced against the underside of the washer by the pressure in the bottle. To open the bottle the stopper is slightly turned; the gas then escapes either through a groove made for the purpose or through spaces i between

the threads, and the pressure being relieved the ball K falls. The washer D may be fixed to the stopper A as shown in Fig. 2, and a groove is made in the neck of the bottle instead of the ledge.

Bottle necks, making.—In forming a bottle neck with an internal screw and a ledge or groove, as shown above, a special tool or pair of tongs is employed. The plug is formed with an external screw, and a ring to correspond with the ledge. It has a bearing in the swiller and is attached to a square rod which has a circular bearing in a cross-piece. A guide attached to one of the legs holds the square rod when the tongs are open, but leaves it free to rotate when they are closed. The bottle is placed in the tongs and rotated by a punty in the ordinary manner, the plug rotating with the bottle and forming the interior of the neck. On now releasing the tongs the guide grips the square rod and prevents the rotation of the plug, and the bottle may be unscrewed from the tongs.

15,281. Rylands, D. Nov. 20.

Bottle necks, making.—Relates to the class of bottles described in Specification No. 5445, A.D. 1883. A hollow nipple A, Fig. 1, larger than there described, is fitted in one part of the mould, and through it works a hollow punch C, which is automatically supplied with water from the passage F. These holes may also be punched after the bottle has been taken from the mould, as shown in Fig. 2. In this case the punch may be simply dipped into cold water.

Washer grooves.—The top edge of the groove for the rubber washer forming a seating for the internal stopper is made to overhang or project inwards slightly as shown in Fig. 3.

15,424. Varley, J. J. Nov. 22.

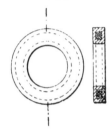

Stoppers.—Relates to washers for internally-stoppered bottles. The rings or seatings, which fit in grooves in the necks of internally-stoppered bottles, are formed of a core of fibrous material coated or covered with india-rubber. A strip of soft india-rubber is first laid round a rod or mandrel and the ends joined. Hempen string or other fibre is wound upon this to form the core and coated with india-rubber in solution. The strip is then folded over and formed into a ring, which is removed from the mandrel, placed in a die, and finished or cured in the usual manner. The die may be dispensed with and the ring cured in chalk or in other known manner.

15,924. Hayslep, F. J., and Morgan, J. Dec. 3.

Stoppers for aërated water bottles. A taper cork, having a groove across the base as shown, is forced into the neck of the bottle until it catches underneath a projecting ledge provided for the purpose. The bottle is opened by forcing the cork in still further with an ordinary opener.

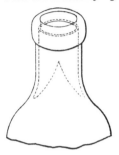

16,374. Codd, H. Dec. 12.

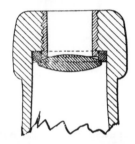

Stoppers for aërated-liquid bottles. A tube or thimble of pewter or like metal screws into the bottle and projects slightly below the overhanging ledge at the bottom of the screw-thread in the neck. An annular recess is thus formed to receive an elastic packing-ring, which forms a seating for a disc of metal, glass, or other hard material.

17,044. Lake, W. R., [*Roorback, W. E., Twitchell, S., and Twitchell, O.*]. Dec. 30.

Stoppers; bottles.—Relates to washers for internally-stoppered bottles, and to means for retaining the stopper while the contents are being poured out. The india-rubber washer C which forms the seat for the stopper is of the form of a double truncated cone, and two depressions are made in the side of the bottle near the bottom, which form two internal shoulders E to hold the stopper when the liquid is being poured out.

1885

361. Creasy, J. T., and **Wild, A. T. J.** Jan. 10.

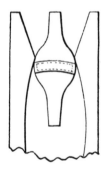

Stoppers, internal. The stopper, formed as shown, has a groove round the middle to hold an elastic ring. The bottle, which may be of any ordinary shape, is easily opened by pressing the top of the stopper to one side.

377. Sharpe, I. R. Jan. 10.

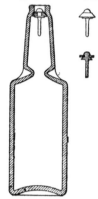

Stoppers, internal, for bottles for aërated liquids. The stopper has a rounded or conical head, round which is a groove to receive a conical or flat india-rubber washer, and a long spindle to prevent the stopper from turning in the neck of the bottle. It fits upon a conical seating formed for the purpose in the neck, which may also have projections to prevent the stopper from falling to the bottom.

1466. Mayall, R. Feb. 3.

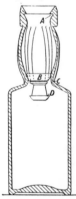

Bottle necks; stoppers; opening internally-stoppered bottles.—The bottle and stopper of the form

54

indicated are used for beer or other non-aërated liquids. The neck of the bottle is corrugated, and preferably oval in section, and has a recess A to receive a conical india-rubber washer B on the stopper, which is first inserted by an instrument similar to an ordinary opener for internally-stoppered bottles. When required to be opened, the stopper is pushed still further into the bottle, but is prevented from falling to the bottom by the contraction C. The neck being sufficiently large in the middle to allow it to turn, it can be extracted by nippers with a divided rim which catch under the ledge D.

2301. Codd, H. Feb. 19.

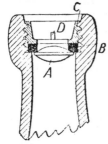

Stoppers, internal, for bottles containing aërated liquids. The disc A of strong tough material, preferably glass, is forced by the gaseous pressure against the elastic ring B. This ring is held upon a ledge at the bottom of a screw-thread on the interior of the neck by a screw tube or ferrule C. A small projection D is provided to fit into a corresponding hollow in the key used for screwing the tube into or out of place.

3935. Walker, W. G. March 27.

Stoppers, internal. Wooden internal bottle stoppers of the form shown (A being the wooden stem

and B an india-rubber ring) are weighted by pouring molten metal into a recess C at the end of a hole D,

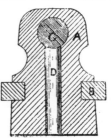

bored longitudinally as shown or in any other direction. The hole is filled up by a wooden plug to prevent any action of the liquid on the metal.

3936. Walker, W. G. March 27.

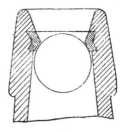

Stoppers, internal. Solid or hollow glass ball bottle stoppers are subjected to a grinding process over the whole surface to obviate the difficulty arising from the ridge in the former and the irregularity of shape in the latter.

4246. Rylands, D. April 7.

Opening   internally-stoppered bottles; stoppers.—Fig. 2 is a sectional plan on the line *b b*, Fig. 1. A ring *f* is capable of turning, and when in the position shown in Fig. 2 an india-rubber projection *g* completely closes a hole *e* in the neck of bottle. By turning the ring *f* the hole is uncovered so that the pressure is relieved and the ball falls down. The hoop or ring *f* and the neck of the

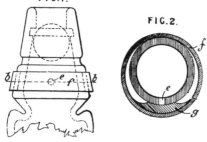

FIG.1.

FIG.2.

bottle, or the neck alone, may be formed elliptical, in which cases the part *g* may be continuous; or the parts may be circular and concentric and four projections *g* used.

6002. Wilkinson, J. May 15.

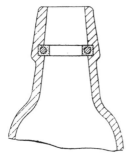

Stoppers, internal, washers for. The washer in internally-stoppered bottles is made of two parts, an external soft rubber portion and an internal portion of comparatively inelastic material, such as soft metal, hard rubber, &c. The washer is introduced into the bottle and expanded into its searing by passing a cone into it.

6384. Rylands, D. May 26.

Bottles; stoppers; opening internally-stoppered bottles.—The bottle D has an internally screwed

mouthpiece L, which screws on to a rubber washer K against which the internal stopper B presses when the bottle is filled. A groove is cut in the

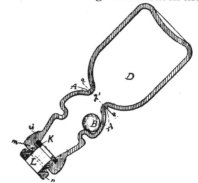

screw-thread *m* to allow of the release of the pressure in the bottle for opening purposes when the head *n* is turned very slightly. This invention consists in the combination of this form of bottle stopper with contractions and indentations in the bottle neck to hold the stopper when pouring out the liquid.

10,997. Codd, H. Sept. 16.

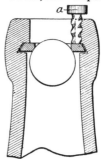

Opening internally-stoppered bottles.—A pin *a*, which may be screwed or plain, is fitted at the side of the neck as shown. It bears against the washer so that a slight movement downwards displaces the washer, when the pressure is released and the ball falls.

12,377. Codd, H. Oct. 16.

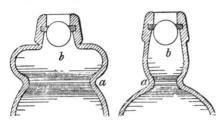

Bottles.—The necks are made of the form shown, which are sections at right-angles to one another. The bottle is only filled up to *a*, and the space *b* prevents undue pressure of gas when the temperature rises. The stoppers may be screw, ball, or any usual form.

13,158. Vallet, L. Oct. 31.

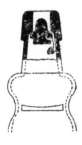

Stoppers, internal. Consists in the combination with a bottle having a bulbous neck of an internal stopper, having a rubber washer, which is inserted complete from the outside. Stoppers of the required type are described in Specifications No. 490, A.D. 1875, and No. 13, 157, A.D. 1885.

14,069. Codd, H. Nov. 17.

Bottles; stoppers.—In bottles for aërated liquids, the necks are of the form shown, Fig. 2 being a section across the neck on the line *x*. and Fig. 1 a vertical section of the bottle. In pouring, the ball is allowed to drop into one of the side compartments *a, a* to be out of the way. In filling, the ball is transferred to

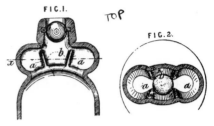

the centre *b* and, on removing the bottle from the filling machine, the ball is forced by gas pressure to the position shown in Fig. 1.

14,339. Edwards, J. Nov. 23.

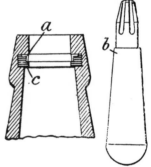

Stoppers.—Relates to means for fixing the washers of internal stoppers for aërated-water bottles. A tin washer *a*, of rather smaller internal diameter than the india-rubber washer *c*, is placed in the position shown, by the tool *b*, and so secures the rubber washer in position.

14,755. Samson, W. Dec. 1.

Stoppers.—Internal stoppers are made conical and weighted at their larger ends. They are softened by soaking &c., so that they may be forced through the contracted neck *b*.

15,861. Deeks, J. Dec. 24.

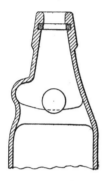

Bottles; stoppers.—The bottle is contracted at the base of the neck so that the stopper cannot fall into the bottle, and a hemispherical recess is formed at one end of this contraction only, instead of at both ends as described in Specification No. 2212, A.D. 1871.

16,057. Day, J. M. Dec. 31.

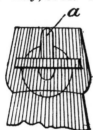

Opening internally-stoppered bottles; stoppers.—A groove is formed in the side of the neck of a bottle for aërated liquids in which a pin *a* fits which passes through the

washer. The pressure is released by moving the top of the pin towards the centre of the neck and thus displacing the washer.

1886

305. Sullivan, W. Jan. 8.

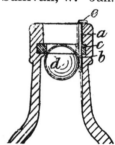

Stoppers; opening internally-stoppered bottles; venting bottles.— A tube *a*, closed at the top end and formed with a lateral orifice *b*, passes through the washer *c* of a ball-stoppered bottle. On pulling up the tube so that the orifice comes above the washer, gas can escape, thereby allowing the ball *d* to fall. A projection *e* on the top of the tube assists in pulling it up, and for greater safety the tube *a* may lie in a vertical groove, as shown. The tube may be replaced by a solid pin which is pulled out of the washer to vent the bottle.

1549. Codd, H. Feb. 2.

Bottles, labels or marking devices for. A suitable device is printed on the outside edge of the washer used in internally-stoppered bottles so as to show through the glass. Or a ring of printed or embossed metal or other material may be placed in the groove before the washer is inserted.

1811. Rylands, D. Feb. 8.

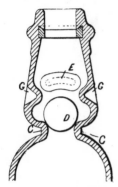

Stoppers; bottles.—To prevent the ball D from falling back into the bottle the neck is nipped at the bottom at C; internal projections E are made to prevent the ball from rolling into the mouth while pouring, and also other projections G, at right-angles to the former, to prevent the ball D from jamming the rotating brush used in cleaning the bottle.

8650. Varley, J. J. July 1,

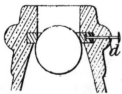

Opening internally-stoppered bottles; stoppers, internal. A push-piece *d* fits through the side of the neck for displacing the washer; it may take various forms. The washer and stopper may be perforated or channelled.

14,661. Rylands, D. Nov. 12.

Bottles with means for retaining stoppers when pouring. The contraction *c* at the base of the neck, which prevents the ball *s* from falling into the bottle, is inclined upward towards the projections *p* which retain the ball when pouring.

14,720. Rylands, D. Nov. 13.

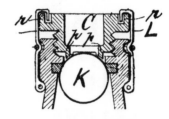

Stoppers; opening internally-stoppered bottles.—A screw plug C or cap is provided with projections *p* which force the stopper K from its seating when the plug is screwed ·down. Hooked lugs L are secured to the bottle neck in any suitable manner and take into a groove *r* in the screw plug C to prevent it from being removed.

14,991. Parsell, R. Nov. 18.

Bottles; opening internally-stoppered bottles; stoppers.—The bottle is cast with a ring *a* round the centre, or in any suitable position, to hold it on a shelf in the case. A vertical hole admits a pin *b* which is used to depress the washer to allow gas to escape and the stopper to fall. A floating ball stopper is used made

59

of vulcanite or other suitable material.

15,883. Richardson, J. Dec. 4.

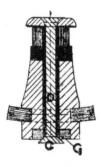

Stoppers, internal. Consists in providing internal bottle stoppers with relief valves to facilitate unstoppering. A special form is shown. A spindle D of triangular section works in a hole of circular section, and is provided with a flange C which closes against the rubber washer G.

1887

649. Rylands, D. Jan. 15. [*Complete Specification but no Letters Patent.*]

Opening internally-stoppered bottles; stoppers, bottle necks for. A relief valve P is placed in the side of the neck which is opened and closed by turning the level R.

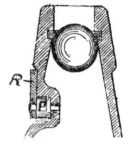

876. Rylands, D. Jan. 20. [*Complete Specification but no Letters Patent.*]

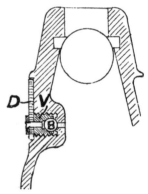

Opening internally-stoppered bottles; stoppers, bottle necks for. Relates to relief valves for internally-stoppered bottles. The screw plug V is grooved so as to allow freer egress to the gas, and is operated by the lever D, the movement of which is limited to 180°. In the form shown the perforation is closed by a spherical rubber valve B, but various forms may be given to this part, as also to the screw plug, which in some cases may have only a portion of a thread formed on it, The grooves are sometimes formed in the thread in the neck instead of on the plug.

998. Rylands, D., and **Boughton, H. F.** Jan. 22.

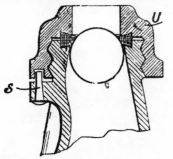

Stoppers, internal. The washer is held in a dovetailed groove formed partly in the bottle neck and partly in the loose screw-piece U, the movement of which is limited by a stop S in various ways, one of which is shown.

4250. Rylands, D. March 22.

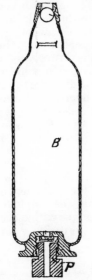

Bottles; stoppers.—In the foot of the internally-stoppered bottle B is placed a perforated valve stopper P constructed as shown, with a cross-cut on its end so as to allow a portion of the contents of the bottle to be withdrawn without loss of gas from that which remains. The position and shape of the plus P may be varied, and in one form the internal stopper is dispensed with, the perforated plug then being used for filling and withdrawing; in this case the washer is cemented to the top of the plug

9771. Rylands, D. July 12.

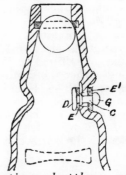

Venting bottles; opening internally-stoppered bottles.— Relates to a release valve consisting of a stud C carrying two washers E, E[1], the inner one E being the same size as the head D; the head G is of such a size as will allow of the stud being inserted from the inside of the bottle. The valves are specially applicable to the bottles described in Specification No. 348, A.D. 1885. For building up the valve the washer E is picked up by a pointer, and by means of a suitable presser is forced over the pointer on to the stud C against the head D. A long instrument, trough-shaped on its upper side, and having a lever device, then carries the valve into the bottle mouth and passes the stud through the hole in the neck, after which the washer E[1] is put on by means of the pointer and presser.

11,036. Foster, F. Aug. 12.

Stoppers; bottle necks, making.— The mouth of an internally-stoppered bottle is formed with a corrugated surface B, by which means a disc may be easily held in the neck above the stopper, thus obviating labelling over the neck to avoid an accumulation of dust. The corrugations are formed by a corrugated collar fitted on the plug of the tongs. When it is desired to fit the · washer with a lever B for displacing the same, one or more of the corrugations are carried to a greater depth, in which case the remainder of the surface may be plain.

11,638. Rylands, D. Aug. 27.

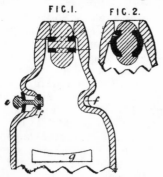

Stoppers; bottles.—Relates to internal stoppers for bottles formed with contractions *g*, indentations *f*, *f*, and with or without a relief valve *e*, and two additional indentations above the contractions *g*, such as are described in Specifications No. 5445, A.D. 1883, No. 348, A.D. 1885, and No. 1811, A.D. 1886. The stoppers are formed so that either end will form a perfect closure. In that shown in Fig. 1 two washers are used; a modified form consists in one washer placed centrally. A third form is that shown in Fig 2.

12,453. Walton, F. A. [*trading as* C. F. Palmer & Co.]. Sept. 14.

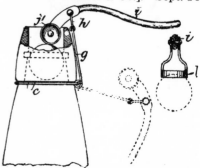

Opening internally-stoppered bottles.—The opener is permanently attached to the bottle, and consists of a lever *i* connected to a ring *c* round the bottle neck by links *g*, *h*. Two dished revolving discs *j¹* are attached to the short end of the lever, and serve to displace the stopper. Or a cupped depressor *l* may be used. The short link *h* may be dispensed with, or the depressor may be pivoted to the lever between the handle and fulcrum, or the lever may be slotted. According to the Provisional Specification, a screw cap or plug for depressing the stopper may be employed; in this case it engages with a screw thread formed on the inside or outside of the bottle neck.

14,941. Barrett, H., and **Varley, J. J.** Nov. 2.

Stoppers; opening internally-stoppered bottles.—Relates to means for facilitating opening internally-stopped bottles. The flattened ends *f* of a bow wire *e* are

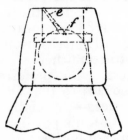

held between the washer and the edge of the washer groove, so that by moving the bow to the other side of the neck the washer is distorted, and the gas escapes.

1888

8595. Samson, W. June 12.

Stoppers.—Internal stoppers are shaped as shown and formed from

cork and weighted with lignum-vitae, porcelain, &c., so as always to float with the narrow end upper-most. To insert the stoppers into the bottles they are softened by soaking in hot water or by other means, and then compressed.

16,436. Vallet, L. Nov. 13.

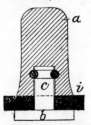

Stoppers, internal. The head *a* is made of a hard material, such as glass or china, and is of less diameter than the base *b*, which is made of a yielding material such as wood. A washer *i* is carried between the two parts, various ways of connecting which are described, such as a key of molten metal or shellac, &c. A relief valve to facilitate opening may be provided in the centre of the bottle stopper.

It is significant that 1888 produced only two minor innovations related to internally-stoppered bottles. The industry's age of invention was drawing to a close. Sales were to reach a peak within a few years—followed by inevitable progress towards those screw-stoppered bottles familiar to all diggers who worked on sites dated later than 1895.

After 1888 Hiram Codd's patents on his 'Original' bottle expired. The bottle could now be made by any bottlemaker without payment of a licence fee, a situation that produced an abundance of copies bearing embossing including the words, 'Codd's expired patent'. Many firms turning out these expired patents were small companies with few overheads and able to produce their wares at prices which might have spelled ruin for Dan Rylands' Barnsley empire where the production of globe-stoppered bottles kept thousands of men and women employed. Fortunately for present-day collectors the break-up of the Codd-Rylands partnership in 1884 encouraged Dan Rylands to greater inventiveness. He still had cast-iron patent protection on his 'Crystal Valve' bottle and there were large numbers of mineral water makers who preferred his 'Reliance', 'Acme' and 'Empress' bottles to the 'Original'. Although he was obliged to reduce prices—especially on the 'Original'—he was still able to maintain his position as the world's major supplier of globe-stoppered bottles.

He also had an ace up his sleeve—the clever idea of adding coloured lips to the mouths of mineral water bottles as an aid to identification which, it was hoped, would deter the widespread practice of stealing bottles that went on in the trade. The following extract from Rylands' 1889 catalogue explains this new patent:

'New style of marking bottles. One of the greatest grievances of a large mineral water manufacturer at the present day is the continual loss of bottles, quantities of which are either stolen and re-sold by hawkers, or accidentally mixed with those of other manufacturers of the same town. Great pains have been taken to have bottles carefully lettered, or even made in a peculiar fashion, but with all these precautions this grievance of lost bottles still extensively prevails, to the great annoyance of the owners. We have therefore obtained a patent for colouring certain portions of any bottle, by which means a mineral water manufacturer can detect his bottles at a considerable distance, without the trouble of having to look whether his name is engraved upon them. Any mineral water manufacturer who adopts these bottles will be able to easily distinguish them anywhere. To accomplish this object we make the mouth portion of the bottle any of the colours mentioned below, the remaining portion of the bottle being of ordinary pale glass. In addition to affording a very effective mark these distinctively coloured mouths greatly increase the attractiveness of the bottle. It will at once be seen that we cannot in justice to our customers make the same coloured mouth for two manufacturers in the same town and we undertake never to do this so long as we have dealings with firms in the same town. Of course we shall consider ourselves at liberty to make any colour for different makers, but on no account shall we use the same colour for two makers in any one district. The usual colours available are blue, amber and green, the price for coloured mouths being two shillings per gross in addition to the ordinary price.'

It was Rylands' patent protection on coloured lips which forced other makers of globe-stoppered bottles to produce their wares in brown, amber, dark green, blue and even black glass. In addition to providing late nineteenth century mineral water makers with easily identifiable and more attractive bottles, these completely coloured specimens provide today's collectors with some of their most prized specimens.

1892

1418. Allen, G. W. J., and **Creswell, J.** Jan. 25.

FIG.6.

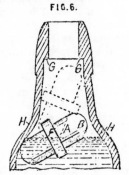

Stoppers.—The stopper consists of a light cylindrical body A, having rounded ends B, and a central annular groove to receive an elastic ring F. The bottle has a ledge G to form a seating for the stopper, and sloping shoulders H to guide it into the neck.

2146. Bedford, T. Feb. 4.

Stoppers.—For internal bottle stoppers, the india-rubber ring is

dispensed with, and a ferrule C, of cork, wood, "woodite," vulcanite, &c., is screwed or cemented into the neck. The ferrule may be also held in

FIG.1.

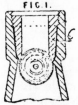

position by a screwed plug or cap having a corresponding perforation through its centre.

5085. Benson, H. March 15.

FIG.1.

Stoppers; opening internally-stoppered bottles.—Internal stoppers are made of the shape shown in Fig. 1, provided with a central perforation through which passes a rod 2 having washers 3 in grooves near each end. For opening the bottle the rod is depressed till the lower washer is forced away from the stopper; the compressed gas escapes by the sides of the rod, and the stopper falls into the bottle.

7662. Hughes, S. April 23.

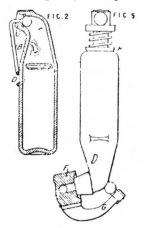

Bottles for containing aërated liquids are made with the orifice at the side, by bending the neck, as shown, or by having a raised orifice made in the side of the neck and the end closed. The bottle is closed in the ordinary way by an internal ball.

Opening internally-stoppered bottles.—A metal, &c. rod B, Fig. 2, bent at the end C, is provided with an eye &c. D, bent to fit to the side of the bottle. By placing the appliance in the position shown, and grasping it and the bottle, the internal stopper can be forced from its seat.

Bottling.—In machines for filling the bottles described, the cup F, Fig 5, for receiving the neck or orifice of the bottle, is placed to one side in an inclined position as shown, and an arm or rest G is provided for suppor-

ting the bottle, which is held in position by a disc or pad H in the usual way.

16,366. Tipping, H. Sept. 13.

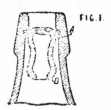

Stoppers.—Relates to internal stoppers for bottles containing aërated liquids. The stopper is made of elongated form, so that it does not readily enter the neck when emptying the bottle. A knob is formed on one end, which is adapted to sit on the washer in the neck, and the other end may be tapered to cylindrical, or may also be formed with a knob. When tapered or cylindrical the rail may be made sufficiently long to prevent the stopper turning in the bottle. Various forms, hollow or solid, may be used; that shown in Fig. 1 has knobs A, B at the ends, either of which is adapted to close the bottle. The Provisional Specification states that for siphon bottles the stopper is made to serve as a tube, through which the liquid is delivered, a valve in the stopper head being actuated by a lever, &c. in the siphon head.

1893

19,650. Henderson, W. Oct. 19.

Stoppers; opening internally-stoppered bottles.—The stopper B has a shank P fixed on each side so that both sides of the stopper may come into use. The bottle is opened by pressing the uppermost shank sideways or inwards.

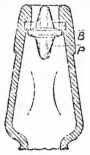

24,143. Hill, S. Dec. 15.

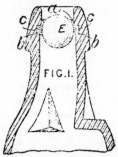

FIG.1.

Stoppers.—The internal stopper E is made sufficiently small to pass freely into the bottle neck, and the india-rubber &c. washer C, which is inserted in the groove *b* in the neck after the stopper has been introduced, is formed with an annular ring or fillet *d* which prevents the stopper from again leaving the bottle. The stopper may be made of a material which will float, in which case the bottle can be filled in an upright position.

1894

19,078. Jones, J. Oct. 8.

Stoppers.—The internal glass stopper A is of slightly tapered form, as shown, the tapered part A[1] being ground to fit the tapered seating B[1] in the neck of the bottle &c. The neck is formed with a channel C terminating in a pocket C[1], the pocket being adapted to receive the stopper when the bottle &c. is opened to

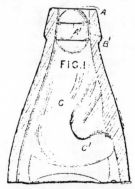

FIG.1

permit the free escape of the contents. The channel C and pocket C[1] are made sufficiently narrow to prevent the stopper from turning endways within the neck.

1895

5615. Brooke, W. March 18.

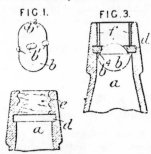

FIG 1.   FIG. 3.

Stoppers.—Relates to bottles which are stoppered internally, and is to facilitate the introduction and removal of the stopper after the bottle is made. As shown in Fig. 1, the bottle neck *a* is screw-threaded internally, and the stopper *b*, which is of elongated form, is formed with helically arranged projections b^1, or with a screw thread, adapted to engage with the screw-thread e in the neck. The stopper is also formed with recesses b^2, or with suitable projections, so that it can be readily turned by a suitable key or by the fingers. To insert the stopper, it is screwed through the part e until it falls inserted in the groove d. The stopper can be removed by first removing the washer and then screwing the stopper in the reverse direction through the part e.

23,559. Boult, A. J., [*Thomas, F. R. H.*]. Dec. 9.

FIG.2.

Stoppers.—Ball stoppered bottles are made with a comparatively short and widely flared neck c^1, the ball being retained during pouring by a square shoulder B of a width not less than the radius of the ball. The seating ring d is placed close to the mouth. The resulting short neck lessens the risk of breakage.

1896

1539. Blakemore, C., and **Chandler, J.** Jan. 22.

Stoppers.—Relates to internal stoppers for bottles containing aërated liquids. The stopper b, Fig. 1, is formed with central passage a, which is normally closed by the valve c, held on its seat by the spring e. In opening the bottle, the pressure is first reduced by raising the valve by means of the knob f. The valve

also opens automatically, in case of excessive pressure within the bottle, and so prevents the bottle bursting. In a modification, the valve is arranged to close the inner end of the passage a. In another form, the valve consists of a flat spring arranged to lie over the outer end of

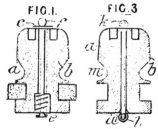

FIG.I. FIG.3

the passage A. In the form shown in Fig. 3, the valve consists of an india-rubber ball k connected by an elastic strand m to a similar ball l, or to the base of the stopper &c. When the ball l is employed, bye-passages a^1 are formed in the stopper to permit the escape of gas, or the ball itself may be perforated.

21,721. Walker, T. H., and **Soar, G.** Oct. 1.

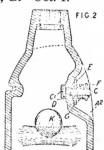

FIG.2

Bottles; opening internally-stoppered bottles.—Relates to means for facilitating the opening of internally-stoppered bottles containing aërated liquids. The neck of the bottle is formed with a gas passage at the bottom of a recess A^2, the passage being normally closed by the valve C^1 and washer D, which are held in place by means of the nut F, spring G, and washer E on the screwed stem C of the valve. In opening the bottle, the nut F is unscrewed and the valve is pressed inward, until the gas is released sufficiently to allow the stopper K to fall from its seat.

Although many 'expired patents'—Codd's, Rylands' and others—could have been manufactured without payment of fees to patentees by bottlemakers of the 1890's few availed themselves of the opportunity. Public tastes were changing rapidly and improved standards of hygiene had begun to cast doubts on the suitability of stoppers that fell into the contents when bottles were opened. But many mineral water makers, especially those in country districts, soldiered on with internal stoppers well into the twentieth century and there were sparks of renewed interest with such patents as Beavis' of 1897 which, it was claimed, reduced the risk of damage to the internal walls of the neck caused by the falling marble. Further proof that marble bottles were still fairly widely used in the late nineteenth century is given in Meredith's patent of 1899 which suggests a deterrent to the practice by small boys of breaking bottles to obtain free marbles.

1897

665. Connor, J. Jan. 9.

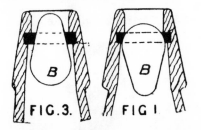

Stoppers.—Relates to internal stoppers for aërated-water bottles. The stopper B is made egg-shaped, as shown, to prevent the wilful breakage of the bottle to obtain the stopper for use as a marble. Either end of the stopper may be used to effect the closure of the bottle.

3349. Pollard, A. R. Feb. 8.

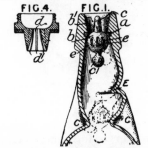

Bottles &c.; stoppers; bottling.—The neck of the bottle or the like is provided with a washer *a* to form a seat for the internal stopper *b*. The stopper is formed with a projection *c* and a counter-balance c^1, the projection *c*, when the stopper is in the closing position, being nearly flush with the mouth.

69

Grooves *e* are also formed in the stopper, and the neck is formed with indentations C, E, which respectively prevent the stopper from falling into the bottle &c., and from obstructing the mouth when pouring out the contents. In opening the vessel, the stopper is tilted to one side, as shown in dotted lines at b^1, by pressing the projection *c*, this operation permitting the escape of the gas through the grooves *e*. When the internal pressure is sufficiently reduced, the stopper falls away from the washer *a*. The bottling-machine used for filling bottles closed by these stoppers is provided with a conical nozzle *d*, Fig. 4, which serves to centre the projection *c* in the neck, the nozzle being also formed with grooves d^1 to permit the passage of the liquid into the bottle.

26,359. Beavis, C. E. Nov. 12.

FIG 2.

Bottle necks.—The stopper-retaining indent A of an internally-stoppered aërated water bottle is made of curved form, as shown, so as to form with the indent B a curved channel C for the stopper. It is stated that the invention prevents 'starring' or fracture of the bottle by the oscillation of the stopper, or by the wedging of the stopper by the brush of the bottle-washing machine, and also facilitates the return of the stopper to its seat after filling.

24,649. Martin, J. Oct. 25.

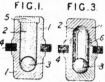

FIG.I.   FIG.3

Stoppers.—Relates to wooden internal stoppers for aërated water bottles &c., the stopper 1 being made of lignum vitae &c., and formed with a longitudinal cavity 2 to receive the weight 3. This weight is preferably spherical, and by rolling to the lowest end of the stopper serves to enter the latter in its proper position into the neck after filling. In Fig. 1, the end of the stopper is closed by a screw or other plug 5 after the weight has been inserted. In Fig 3, the stopper is made in two parts secured together by a screw or other joint 6, the washer 4 being held between opposing shoulders on the two parts. The shoulders may be dispensed with, in which case the washer serves as a distance-piece between the parts of the stopper.

1898

4355. Forshaw, J. Feb. 22.

Stoppers.—Relates to internal bottle stoppers, which are aërated in the neck after filling by a leaden weight free to roll in a cavity in the stopper. In the present invention, the weight *b* is enclosed in the cylindrical chamber *a* in the stopper, the open end of the chamber being formed with an undercut recess d^1 to receive the closing-plug f. This plug is formed of a suitable hard but expansible material, such as poplar wood, and is compressed into the recess d^1. When the plug subsequently becomes moistened, it expands within the recess so that it cannot be withdrawn.

4657. Forshaw, J. Feb. 25.

Stoppers.—Relates to internal bottle stoppers, which are weighted at the head, to ensure that they shall fall head foremost into the necks after the bottles have been filled. In the present invention, the head of the stopper is formed with a cavity b, which is partially filled with lead &c., and is then closed by a plug d of poplar wood, cork, &c. The plug is compressed into the constricted mouth of the cavity, and, after it becomes moistened, expands so as to key itself therein.

10,725. Connor, J. May 11.

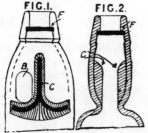

Bottle necks.—The neck of an aërated-water bottle is formed with two opposed internal partitions to prevent the stopper B from blocking the neck during filling. The partitions also serve to prevent the stopper rolling, and act as guides to direct it to its seat F.

22,969. Dixon-Nuttall, F. R. Nov. 1.

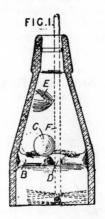

FIG.1.

FIG.2.

Bottles.—In internally-stoppered bottles, the indents B, which prevent the stopper from falling into the body of the bottle, are formed with recesses D, which form a seat for the stopper C to prevent it from rattling when the bottle is empty, and also facilitate the washing or cleaning of the bottle. The recesses are formed a little to one side of the centre, on the side opposite to the stopper-retaining projection E, to facilitate the insertion of an ordinary bottle-cleaning brush F.

26,049. Seyboldt, J. Dec. 9.

FIG.I

Stoppers.—The internal ball stopper 1 is made smaller than the narrowest part of the bottle neck, so that, when the washer 3 is withdrawn, the stopper can be removed from the bottle.

25,626. Braubach, E. A. Dec. 5.

Stoppers.—Relates to the stoppering of bottles containing aërated liquids. The neck is provided with the usual seating and indents for the internal ball stopper *a*. and, in addition, is screw-threaded to receive the external screw stopper *b*, which is provided with a washer *c*. The stopper *b* is made sufficiently long to displace the ball *a* when screwed down, and can then be unscrewed to permit the bottle to be emptied. The bottle can be partially emptied and restoppered. The threads on the stopper *b* and neck may be interrupted.

1899

2727. Meredith, J. Feb. 7.

Stoppers.—To prevent the breakage of internally-stoppered bottles, in order to obtain the stopper for use as a marble, the stopper A is made of elongated shape, with one or both ends spherical. The neck of

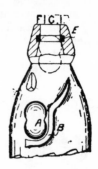

the bottle is formed with indents B, adapted to prevent the stopper from falling into the body of the bottle, and to guide it to its seat on the washer E.

The last patent relating to 'bullet' stoppers was Schmedtje's of 1905.

10,693. Schmedtje, A. H. May 22.

Stoppers, internal.—An internal stopper is formed of a solid glass body with tapered ends 3, 4 ground to fit a ground seating 8 at the mouth of the bottle. The stopper is inserted during the manufacture of the bottle, and is formed with annular grooves 5, 6 to facilitate manipulation. The stopper is held away from its seat while the bottle is inverted and filled, and is then allowed to fall

72

into place, either end up.

The last related to globe-stoppered bottles was Shaw's of 1907.

6875. Shaw, A. March 22.

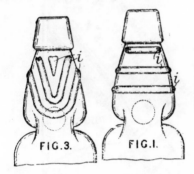

FIG.3.   FIG.I.

Bottles.—Relates to means for strengthening the parts of an aërated-water glass bottle which under ordinary conditions are blown comparatively thin and weak. The moulds are provided with cavities adapted to retard the flow of molten metal and to form ribs, beads, or bars *i* on the neck, the slow flow of the metal tending to thicken the walls of the bottle adjacent to the ribs &c.

Very few specimens of the Adams & Barrett's 1868 patent have been found, the few known specimens coming from early dumps in Jersey and the southern counties of England. Northern dumps of the same age which have been excavated contain only Hamiltons. This suggests Adams & Barrett bottles achieved only localised popularity. Their rarity merits a Price Guide number of *60+*.

BASE EMBOSSING

A half-pint Adams & Barrett bottle found in Sussex. Price guide number: 60+.

Barrett & Elers' 'wooden plug' bottles are found over a much wider area but they certainly qualify as rarities. Those made under licence by Lumb & Co. of Castleford are most frequently encountered (Price guide number: *40*); specimens made by other licencees or by the Barrett & Elers Company are much more difficult to find. (Price guide number: *50+*).

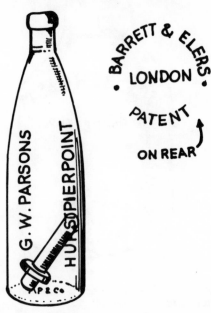

A Barrett & Elers' 'wooden plug' specimen made by Lumb & Co., Castleford. Aqua; approx. 1 pint. Price guide number: 40.

The first licencees for Hiram Codd's globe-stoppered bottle were W. Brooke & Co. of Hunslett and Alexander & Austin of Blaydon. These two companies are known to have made Codd's in 1873 but no specimens bearing their names have been found. Ben Rylands took out a licence to manufacture the bottles in 1874. Specimens embossed with his name are highly prized by collectors. Price guide number: *40-60*, depending on width of body. Hybrid versions bearing Ben Rylands' name are also highly prized. Price guide number: *60*.

Other *early* versions of the Codd embossed 'Codd's Patent', but without the name of a licencee, are less difficult to find. Price guide number: *30*.

A very early Ben Rylands' Codd with extra-wide body. (Known by collectors as a 'dumpy'.) Price guide number: 60.

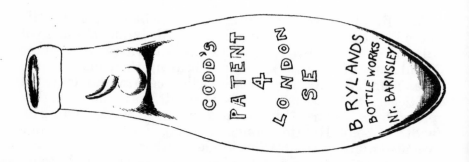

A Ben Rylands' hybrid. Price guide number: 60.

FRONT

CODD'S
PATENT
4
LONDON
S·E·

REAR

B. RYLANDS'
BOTTLE WORKS
NEAR BARNSLEY

An extremely rare Codd made by Ben Rylands in 1877, one year *after* he took Hiram Codd into partnership. Other specimens bearing the same date are embossed 'Rylands & Codd'. A. Hill of Worthing was one of the first mineral water makers to order globe-stoppered bottles in dark green glass. Price guide number of specimens embossed 'B. Rylands' is *60+*. Those embossed 'Rylands & Codd' have a price guide number of *50+*.

Another early Codd without maker's name. Price guide number: 30.

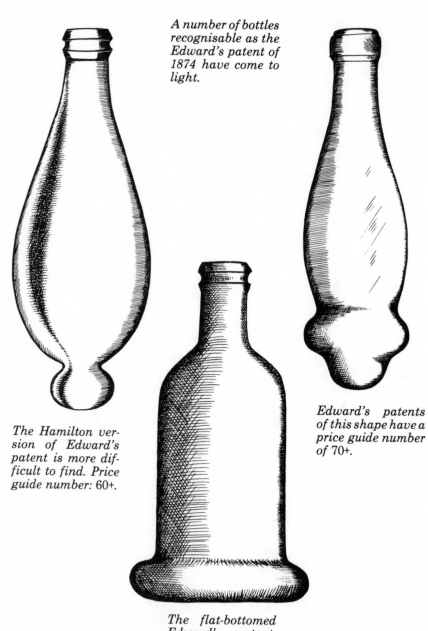

A number of bottles recognisable as the Edward's patent of 1874 have come to light.

The Hamilton version of Edward's patent is more difficult to find. Price guide number: 60+.

Edward's patents of this shape have a price guide number of 70+.

The flat-bottomed Edward's patent. Price guide number: 50+.

Examples of bottles using ball, bullet and plug stoppers which fell to the bottom of the bottle on opening or were trapped in slots and recesses on the body have been found in large numbers. Recognised patents include Sutcliffe's, Lamont's, Aylesbury's, Tapp's, Vernon's, Breffit & Edwards', Sykes-Macvay's, Rose's, Edmond's, Cherry's, Barrett's, Brooke's, Trotman's, Sankey's, Vane's, Ballard's, and Chapman's. Others are unmarked or carry only the name of the bottle maker. (e.g: Adamson, Kilner Bros, Turner.) Their price guide numbers vary between *20* and *40* depending on whether or not their bodies and necks have indentations. Readers who find examples bearing the names of inventors not listed above should note that their bottles are either rare or very localised in distribution. Price guide number: *30+*.

Bullet-stoppered bottle with no body indentations. Price guide number: 20.

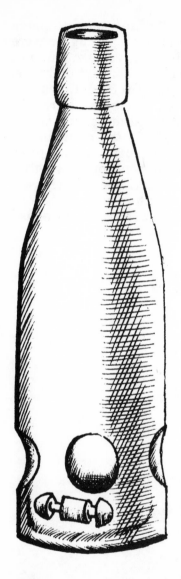 

Bullet-stoppered bottle with body indentations but without inventor's or maker's name. Price guide number: 25.

Bullet-stoppered bottle with neck indentations and inventor's name. (Sutcliffe & Fewings.) Price guide number: 35.

Rare ball-stoppered bottle with body indentation. Inventor and maker unknown. Price guide number: 40.

Bullet-stoppered bottle with embossed design. Inventor and maker unknown. Price guide number: 35.

Post-1880 versions of the 'Original' Codd in aqua are too common to merit inclusion in this price guide. Most, though not all, are embossed 'Codd's expired patent' and they can be found by *any* digger who works a pre-1900 dump. Exceptions include:

Codd's embossed 'Rylands & Codd' which *should* be recognisable by body shape. They were made up to 1881—the year of Ben Rylands' death. (Price guide number: *30+*.)

Codd's embossed 'Codd & Rylands'. They were made between 1881 and 1884 when the Codd-Rylands partnership was dissolved. Price guide number: *25+*.

Codd's embossed 'Hiram Codd, 41 Gracechurch St, London'. They were made by (or for) Hiram Codd after 1884 until his death in 1887. (Price guide number: *25+*.)

Dan Rylands' 'Reliance', 'Acme' and 'Original' Codds in aqua are too common to merit inclusion here but aqua 'Bulb' and 'Empress' Codds deserve a price guide number of *10*.

Dark brown or amber specimens of any of the above rate a price guide number of *30+*.

Dark green specimens of any of the above rate a price guide number of *35+*.

Blue specimens of any of the above rate a price guide number of *50+*.

Black specimens of any of the above rate a price guide number of *100+*.

Coloured lip versions of any of the above rate a price guide number of *40+*, if the body is aqua; *80+* if the body is any other colour.

Rylands' 'Valve' Codds in aqua are rare. Price guide number: *60+*.

Rylands' 'Valve' Codds in brown or amber rate a price guide number of *80+*.

Rylands' 'Valve' Codds in dark green rate a price guide number of *100+*.

Rylands' 'Valve' Codds in blue rate a price guide number of *120+*.

Rylands' 'Valve' Codds in black rate a price guide number of *150+*.

Rylands' 'Valve' Codds in aqua with coloured lips rate a price guide number of *70+*.

Rylands' 'Valve' Codds with coloured lips and bodies in any other colour rate a price guide number of *120+*.

Dark brown specimens of Rylands' 'Reliance', 'Acme' and 'Original' Codds. Price guide number: 30+.

'Bulb' Codd in aqua with
dark green lip. Price guide
number: 40+.

Dark brown Rylands'
'Valve Codd'. Price guide
number: 80+.

Aqua 'Valve' Codd. Price guide number: 60+.

Amber-lipped version of Codd 'Original'. Price guide number: 40+.

Amber - lipped Rylands' 'Valve' Codd. Price guide number: 70+.

Patented globe-stoppered bottles working on similar principles to Hiram Codd's 'Original' which have been found by diggers include the Beavis patent and the Shaw patent. These are fairly common though localised in distribution. They have a price guide number of *15*. A much rarer patent is the Barrett & Elers' version of the 'Original' which has an external screw stopper *in addition* to an internal marble. Price guide number for this specimen is *100+*.

The Beavis patent. Price guide number: 15.

The Barrett & Elers' external screw stopper and internal marble patent. Price guide number: 100+.

Aqua Hamiltons are too common to merit inclusion here but coloured Hamiltons are rare.

Dark green specimens have a price guide number of *35+*.

Brown or amber specimens have a price guide number of *30+*.

Blue specimens have a price guide number of *50+*.

Black specimens have a price guide number of *100+*.

Stoneware Hamiltons are extremely rare. Price guide number: *120+*.

Extra-long *round-bottom* Hamiltons have a price guide number of *15+*. The bottle must be at least fifteen inches long to qualify for this category.

Eight, ten and twelve-sided Hamiltons have a price guide number of *20+*.

Spherical bottles were used by a few mineral water makers for soda water. They have a price guide number of *20* in aqua; *40+* in other colours.

Stoneware Hamilton. Price guide number: 120+.

Extra-long Hamilton (18 ins). Price guide number: 15+.

Spherical soda water (Brown). Price guide number: 40+.

Black glass Hamilton. Price guide number: 100+.

Hybrid (i.e. pointed-bottom) versions of some of the aforementioned globe-stoppered bottles have been found. Aqua specimens embossed 'Codd's expired patent' are most common and have a price guide number of *40+*.

All other hybrids in aqua have a price guide number of *80+*.

Flat-bottom Hamilton hybrids have a price guide number of *90+*.

Aqua specimens with coloured lips have a price guide number of *120+*.

Coloured specimens have a price guide number of *150+*.

Hybrid versions of Rylands' 'Valve' in aqua have a price guide number of *150+*.

Hybrid versions of Rylands' 'Valve' in coloured glass or with coloured lips have a price guide number of *160+*.

Flat-bottomed Hamilton-hybrid. Price guide number: 90+.

Hybrid version of Rylands' 'Reliance' Codd with amber lip. Price guide number: 120.

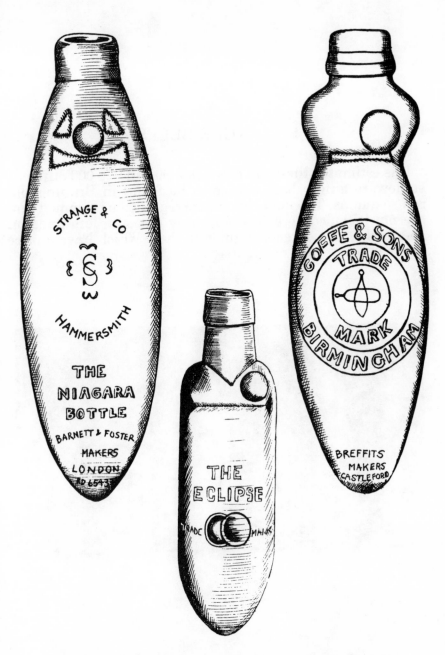

Codd-Hamilton hybrid variations. Price guide number: 80+.

2. GINGER BEERS

It is estimated there are between 5,000 and 10,000 different stoneware ginger beer bottles to be found in Britain's old refuse dumps. The majority can be regarded as common and are not included here. The following notes on less common specimens give a general guide to those which have a price guide number of 10 or greater.

Specimens with coloured shoulders (blue, red, green, etc.) have a price guide number of 10.

Specimens with blue, red or green bodies have a price guide number of 15.

Tall specimens of 'champagne bottle' shape have a price guide number of 12, but if they also have pictorial transfers the price guide number rises to 15.

Left and Above. 'Champagne bottle' shape ginger beers with price guide numbers from 12-15.

91

3. INKS

The number of cottage inks now being found by British diggers has greatly increased during the past year. Nevertheless these bottles are still extremely rare. Blue glass varieties have a price guide number of *200*; aqua and stoneware specimens are rated *180*. Two new figurals have come to light recently. The first is a head and shoulders bust of Mr. Gladstone (price guide number: *150*); the second is in the shape of a snail's shell (price guide number: *140*). Both have been found in aqua only.

The number of registry-marked inks found by diggers has

Snail's   shell figural. Price guide number: 140.

Straight-sided umbrella. Price guide number: 20.

Mr.   Gladstone's   figural. Price guide number: 150.

also increased. These specimens have price guide numbers of *40-50*. Further down the price guide scale are tea kettles (*40*); three-siders (*40*); igloos (*30*); and barrels, umbrellas, and cones (all at *20*). Cobalt blue specimens of the commoner shapes (eight-siders, bells, etc.) have a price guide number of *20*. Dark greens and light blues are rated *5-15*.

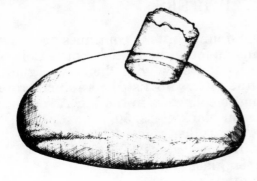

Igloo. Price guide number: 30.

Registry - marked specimen. Price guide number: 40.

Aqua cottage. Price guide number: 180.

93

4. BITTERS

The number of British-found bitters continues to grow slowly but surely. Specimens found by British Bottle Collectors Club members are listed below with their price guide numbers. Readers who find bitters not listed here should rate them at least *30* if selling to collectors in the U.S.A.

Dr. Soule's Hop Bitters in black glass: *50*.
Dr. Doyle's Hop Bitters in amber glass: *40*.
Warner's Safe Bitters in amber glass: *80*.
Bitterquell in olive green glass: *10*.
Hartwig Kantorowicz in milk glass: *20*.
Kent Hop Bitters in black glass: *40*.
Taylor's Perfection Hop Bitters in green glass: *50*.

Dr. Doyle's Hop Bitters in amber glass. Price guide number: 40.

94

Warner's Safe Bitters. Price guide number: 80.

5. SEALED BOTTLES

The British Bottle Collectors Club has compiled a list of all Zara sealed bottles found by members. Price guide numbers for all bottles on the list are as follows:

Drioli and Magazino seals:

(Note: a.l.=applied lip; s.l.=sheared lip; r.l.=re-annealed lip.)

MINIATURES:	Aqua	a.l.; round	...	*45.*
		r.l.; round	...	*45.*
		s.l.; round	...	*55.*
	Zara blue	a.l.; round	...	*45+.*
		r.l.; round	...	*45+.*
		s.l.; round	...	*55.*
	Aqua	a.l.; square	...	*35.*
		r.l.; square	...	*35.*
		s.l.; square	...	*55.*
	Zara blue	a.l., square	...	*35+.*
		r.l.; square	...	*35+.*
		s.l., square	...	*55.*
SMALL:	Aqua	a.l.; round	...	*35+.*
		r.l.; round	...	*35+.*
		s.l.; round	...	*50.*
	Zara blue	a.l.; round	...	*35+.*
		r.l.; round	...	*35+.*
		s.l.; round	...	*50+.*
	Aqua	a.l.; square	...	*35.*
		r.l.; square	...	*35.*
		s.l.; square	...	*50.*
	Zara blue	a.l.; square	...	*35.*
		r.l.; square	...	*35.*
		s.l.; square	...	*50.*
LARGE:	Aqua	a.l.; round	...	*35+.*
		r.l.; round	...	*35+.*
		s.l.; round	...	*50.*
	Zara blue	a.l.; round	...	*35+.*
		r.l.; round	...	*35+.*

				s.l.; round	...	*50.*
Aqua	...	...	...	a.l., square	...	*35.*
				r.l.; square	...	*35.*
				s.l.; square	...	*50.*
Zara blue	...	...	...	a.l.; square	...	*35.*
				r.l.; square	...	*35.*
				s.l.; square	...	*50.*

Luxardo seals: Add 5 to all above price guide numbers. Stampali and Millilich seals: Add 10 to all above price guide numbers.

Other makers: Add 15 to all above price guide numbers.

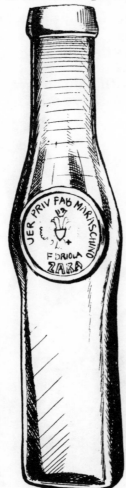

A Drioli Zara sealed bottle; small; aqua; applied lip; square. Price guide number: 35.

97

'Onion' sealed bottles are highly prized and rate a price guide number of *200+*.

Squat cylindrical specimens earlier than 1850 have a price guide number of *180+*.

Later black glass specimens with *body* seals have a price guide number of *100+*.

Those with *shoulder* seals have a price guide number of *80+*.

Two and three-piece mould specimens have price guide numbers from *50-70*.

Turn-mould specimens have price guide numbers from *50-60*.

Continental seals—usually in shades of green—have a price guide number of *40+*.

Square sealed bottles, other than case gins, have a price guide number of *80+*.

Sealed bottles with 'ribbon' seals and those bearing the words 'Imperial Pint' have price guide numbers of *60-70+*.

'Onion' sealed bottle. Price guide number: 200+.

Pre-1850 cylindrical sealed bottle. Price guide number: 180+.

Body sealed specimens. Price guide number: 100+

Square sealed bottle. Price
guide number: 80+.

'Ribbon' seal. Price guide
number: 60+.

6. CASE GINS AND SCHNAPPS

There has been an increase during the past year in the number of shoulder sealed case gins recovered from British dumps but these bottles are still rarities. Early pre-1860s specimens have a price guide number of *70+*; later mould-blown specimens are rated *60+*. Pictorially embossed specimens are equally rare. Price guide number *70+*.

Schnapps bottles have a price guide number of *10* unless they are miniatures which are rated *30*.

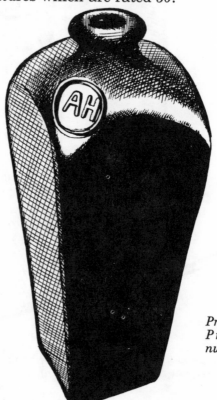

Pre-1860 case gin.
Price guide
number: 70+.

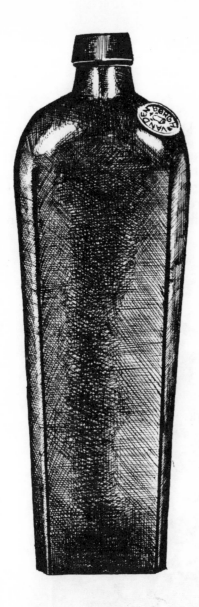 

Mould-blown sealed case gin. Price guide number: 60+.

Pictorially embossed case gin. Price guide number: 70+.

7. BLACK WHISKIES, SELTZERS AND GINGER BEERS

Many collectors have specialised in black glass during the past few years and all black bottles are in demand. Whisky bottles in this group have price guide numbers from *15-25* if cylindrical in body shape and from *25-35* if oval, square or oblong. 'Dumpy' seltzers and black glass ginger beers are also rated up to *35* if embossed.

Oval black glass whisky.
Price guide number: 35.

Black glass ginger beer. Price guide number: 35.

Dumpy Seltzer. Price guide number: 35.

Mould-blown cylindrical whisky. Price guide number: 15.

Free-blown cylindrical whisky. Price guide number: 25.

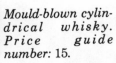

8. FIRE GRENADES

Eight different fire grenades have now been found by members of the British Bottle Collectors Club. They are listed below with price guide numbers:

Harden's Star; spherical; blue. Price guide number: *50*.
Harden's Star; spherical; aqua. Price guide number: *40*.
Harden's Star; spherical; amber. Price guide number: *60*.
Harden's Star; spherical; dark brown. Price guide number: *60*.
Harden's Tubular; blue. Price guide number: *80*.
Minimax Tubular; blue. Price guide number: *50*.
Imperial; spherical; blue. Price guide number: *50*.
Imperial; spherical; dark green. Price guide number: *60*.

Harden's Star; spherical; blue. Price guide number: 50.

Imperial grenade; blue.
Price guide number: 50.

Minimax tubular grenade.
Price guide number: 50+.

Harden's tubular grenade. Price guide number: 80.

9. PATENT MEDICINES

The majority of patent medicines are too common to merit inclusion in this book. Rarer items are listed below with price guide numbers. Any cobalt blue, amber, brown or black *embossed* specimen not listed here should be given a price guide number of at least *15* if mould-blown and at least *30* if pontil marked.

Daffy's Elixir; deep aqua. Price guide number: *80*.

Dalby's Carminative; aqua. Price guide number: *30*.

Dr. Rooke's Rheumatic Lixine; cobalt blue. Price guide number: *20*.

Dr. Silby's Solar Tincture; wedge; ice blue. Price guide number: *60*.

Dr. Townsend's Sarsaparilla; aqua. Price guide number: *30*.

Dr. Townsend's Sarsaparilla; aqua; embossed 'The Blood Purifier'. Price guide number: *50*.

Handyside's Blood Purifier; black. Price guide number: *50*.

Handyside's Consumption Cure; black. Price guide number: *50*.

Hood's Sarsaparilla; aqua. Price guide number: *15*.

Madame Girrard's Hair Restorer; amber. Price guide number: *15*.

Mexican Hair Renewer; cobalt blue. Price guide number: *40*.

Price's Patent Candle Co; wedge; cobalt blue. Price guide number: *100*.

Price's Patent Candle Co; wedge; aqua. Price guide number: *60*.

Radam's Microbe Killer; amber. Price guide number: *80*.

Turlington's Balsam; aqua. Price guide number: *50*.

Warner's Safe Cure, London; amber; various sizes. Price guide number: *40-50*.

Warner's Safe Cure, London; olive green; various sizes. Price guide number: *50-60*.

Warner's Safe Nervine; Warner's Safe Kidney and Liver Cure; Warner's Safe Diabetes Cure. Price guide numbers *50-60*.

Warner's embossed 'Melbourne' or 'Rochester'. Price guide numbers as above.

Warner's embossed 'Frankfurt'. Price guide number: *100*.

Miniature Warner's Safe Cures approx 2½ins. tall. Price guide number: *150+*.

Extra large Warner's Safe Cures of approx. 2 pint capacity. Price guide number: *150+*.

Warner's Safe Compound. Price guide number: *50*.

Radam's Microbe Killer; amber. Price guide number: 80.

Daffy's Elixir; deep aqua. Price guide number: 80.

Turlington's Balsam; aqua. Price guide number: 50.

Dalby's Carminative; aqua. Price guide number: 30.

Miniature Warner's Safe Cure; 2½ ins tall. Price guide number: 150+.

Price's Patent Candle Co.; cobalt blue. Price guide number: 100.

PRICE'S GLYCERIN

GOLD MEDALS
PARIS

GRAND PRIZE
PARIS 1889

PRICES PATENT CANDLE CO.

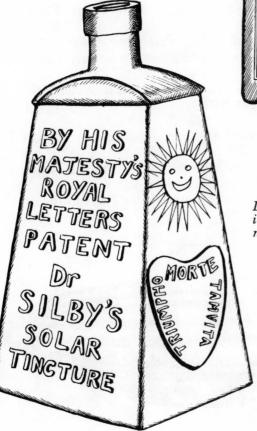

BY HIS MAJESTY'S ROYAL LETTERS PATENT Dr SILBY'S SOLAR TINCTURE

TRIUMPHO MORTE TAM VITA

Dr. Silby's Solar Tincture; ice blue. Price guide number: 60.

10. POISONS

Most poison bottles are very common but those of unusual shapes or with arrows, rats, or 'skull and crossbones' embossing are rare and highly prized by collectors.

'Submarine' shapes; cobalt blue. Price guide: *100+*.

'Submarine' shapes; aqua, dark green or brown. Price guide: *60+*.

'Waisted' shapes; cobalt blue. Price guide: *40+*.

'Waisted' shapes; aqua, dark green or brown. Price guide: *25+*.

Martin patent poison bottles; cobalt blue. Price guide: *60+*.

Martin patent poison bottles; aqua, dark green or brown. Price guide: *35+*.

'Skull and crossbones' embossed specimens; cobalt blue. Price guide: *80+*.

'Skull and crossbones' embossed specimens; aqua, dark green or brown. Price guide number: *40+*.

'Rat' embossed specimens; cobalt blue. Price guide number: *50+*.

'Submarine' poison; cobalt blue. Price guide number: 100+.

Martin patent poison bottle; cobalt blue. Price guide number: 60+.

Skull and crossbones poison; cobalt blue. Price guide number: 80+

Waisted poison bottle; cobalt blue. Price guide number: 40+.

11. GLASS FIGURALS

The very few glass figural bottles which have so far been found in British dumps are highly prized by collectors. Those recovered to date are listed below with price guide numbers. Any other glass figural in aqua, dark green, blue or brown glass found in a pre-1900 dump should be given a price guide number of at least *50*. Modern *clear* glass figurals have little value.

Pistol; sheared lip; aqua. Price guide number: *100+*.
Man in top hat; aqua; sheared lip. Price guide number: *80+*.
Negro boy; aqua; sheared lip. Price guide number: *100+*.
Violin; aqua; sheared lip. Price guide number: *60+*.
Fish; aqua; applied lip. Price guide: *80+*.

Negro boy; aqua. Price guide number: 100+.

Fish; aqua; applied lip. Price guide number: 80+.

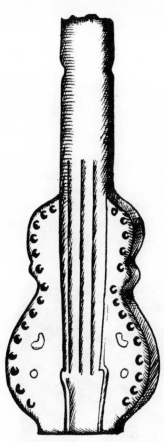

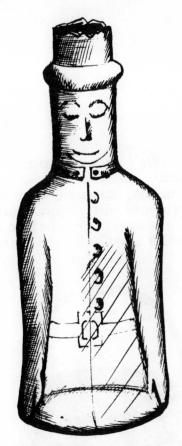

*Violin; aqua. Price guide
number: 60+.*

*Man in top hat; aqua. Price
guide number: 80+.*

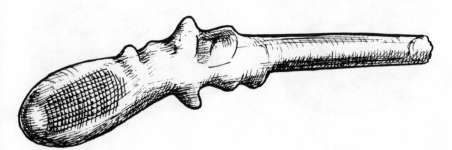

Pistol; aqua. Price guide number: 100+.

12. FAIRY LIGHTS

Fairy lights have recently become very popular collectors' items. Those embossed with abstract patterns are fairly common, but specimens in the shape of flowers and human figures or with pictorial embossing are worthy of inclusion in this book. They can be found in aqua, red, blue, dark green and amber glass. All have a price guide number of *15*.

Above and Right. *Fairy lights. Price guide number:* 15.

13. BABY FEEDERS

The illustrations from nineteenth century wholesale chemists' catalogues below show the three basic shapes found in British dumps.

'Hamilton' shapes have a price guide number of *40+* in clear glass; *60+* in aqua.

Flattened ovals, or 'pancakes', have a price guide number of *20+* in clear glass; *40+* in aqua.

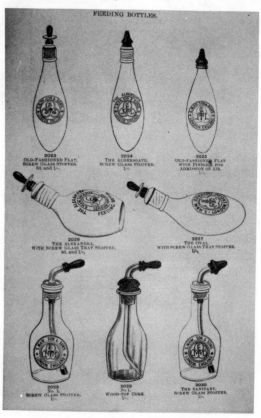

'Stand-up' shapes have a price guide number of *30+* in clear glass; *35+* in aqua.

Blue glass baby feeders are extremely rare. Price guide number: *100+*.

Earthenware baby feeders are also rare. Price guide number: *60+*.

'Pancake' feeder; aqua.
Price guide: 40+.

'Hamilton' shape feeder;
aqua. Price guide number:
60+.

14. OINTMENT POTS

Much interest has been shown recently in these small transfer-printed items, none of which is more than 2½ inches in height. About a dozen different specimens have so far been found by British diggers. All have a price guide number of *15*.

15. CREAM JUGS

This is another group of enthusiastically collected transfer-printed items. When *pictorially* printed these jugs have a price guide number of *10+*. If the printing is in any colour other than black the price guide number rises to *15+*.

16. HOT WATER BOTTLES

Plain specimens have little value, but those decorated with pictorial transfers gave a price guide number of *20+*.

17. HISTORICAL STONEWARE FLASKS AND JUGS

Few of these rare bottles have been found in Victorian refuse dumps. Those owned by British Bottle Collectors Club members have all come from cellars or the dusty shelves of old public houses.

Sir Robert Peel figural; ('Bread for the millions'). Price guide number: *200*.

Daniel O'Connell figural. Price guide number: *200*.

Doulton Mermaid figural. Price guide number: *250*.

Doulton Merboy figural. Price guide number: *250*.

Squirrel figural. Price guide number: *180*.

Punch and Judy flask; ('Triumph of the pen'). Price guide number: *200*.

Albert and Victoria handled flask. Price guide number: *120*.

Bellarmine jugs. Price guide numbers: *120+*.

'*Success to the Mighty Coal Miners*' *Flask. Price guide number:* 200.

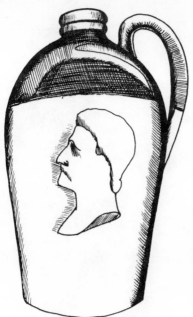

Albert and Victoria handled flask. Price guide number: 120.

Daniel O'Connell figural. Price guide number: 200.

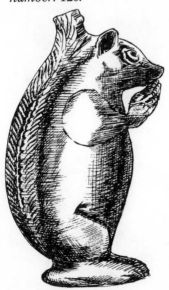

Squirrel figural. Price guide number: 180.

Doulton Mermaid. Price guide number: 250.

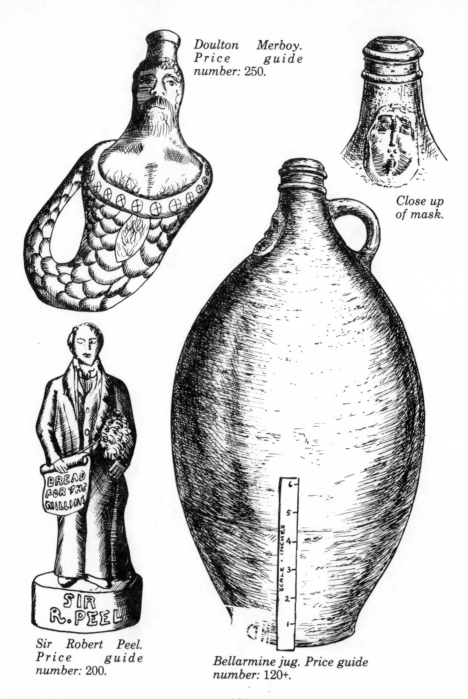

Doulton Merboy. Price guide number: 250.

Close up of mask.

Sir Robert Peel. Price guide number: 200.

Bellarmine jug. Price guide number: 120+.

18. TRANSFER-PRINTED STONEWARE WHISKIES

Interest in bottle collecting has now reached Scotland and Ireland where superb transfer-printed stoneware whisky jugs await determined dump diggers. They have price guide numbers of *60+* when decorated with black transfers and *100+* when decorated with coloured transfers.

19. CLAY TOBACCO PIPES

Only those specimens with bowls in the shape of human heads merit inclusion here. They have price guide numbers of *20+* if the stems are complete; *10+* if stems are incomplete. Readers are warned there are reproduction clay tobacco pipes on the market which are difficult to detect unless one has handled large numbers of genuine Victorian specimens.

20. DOLLS' HEADS AND LIMBS

These are common, but *matching* sets of heads, eyes, arms, and legs which can be used to make reproduction dolls have price guide numbers of *10+*. Boy doll's heads are rare. Price guide number: *20+*.

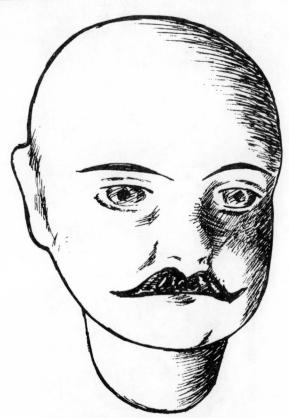

Boy doll's head. Price guide number: 20+.

21. POT LIDS

As a general guide monochrome lids with pictorial transfers have price guide numbers of *30+*.

BIBLIOGRAPHY

The following books and magazines are recommended to readers who wish to improve their knowledge of all aspects of the hobby:

Books.

A Treasure Hunter's Guide, Edward Fletcher, Blandford Press, 1975.
Bottle Collecting, Edward Fletcher, Blandford Press, 1972.
Collecting Pot Lids, Edward Fletcher, Pitman, 1975.
Digging up Antiques, Edward Fletcher, Pitman, 1975.
International Bottle Collectors' Guide, Edward Fletcher, Blandford Press, 1975.
Treasure Hunting For All, Edward Fletcher, Blandford Press, 1973.

Magazines.

Bottles & Relics News, 'Greenacres', Church Rd, Black Notley, Braintree, Essex.
Digger & Collector, 104 Harwal Rd, Redcar, Cleveland.
Old Bottles and Treasure Hunting, 801 Burton Rd, Midway, Burton upon Trent, Staffs.

The quarterly newsletters issued by the British Bottle Collectors Club also contain much useful information. They are available to members only. For details of club membership write to: The National Secretary, British Bottle Collectors Club, 19 Hambro Ave, Rayleigh, Essex.

Note.

Readers who find bottles not included in this guide are asked to send details to me for publication in the above magazines. Readers requesting a private reply *must* include a stamped and addressed envelope. Address: Edward Fletcher, 104 Harwal Road, Redcar, Cleveland.

BOTTLE SHOPS AND DEALERS

Collectors' Old Bottle Room, 184 Main Rd, Biggin Hill, Kent. International Bottle Trader, Box 33, *Bottles & Relics News*, 'Greenacres', Church Rd, Black Notley, Braintree, Essex. The Old Bottle Cellar, 71 Caledonian Rd, London, N.1.